LIFE IN VERSE

Actress **Sheila Hancock** is drawn to poems that deal with our biggest emotional issues: human relationships, love and loss. Following the death of her husband John Thaw in 2002, she found herself reading a collection of Yeats poems he had given her some years earlier. Looking back on her life in recent years, she uncovered an enthusiasm for poets who have explored our deepest feelings, such as Tennyson, Blake and Larkin.

Comedy performer and co-star of *Peep Show* **Robert Webb** fell in love with twentieth-century poetry when a teacher read him T. S. Eliot's 'The Love Song of J. Alfred Prufrock'. His favourite verse embraces modern life in a modern style, whether the love sonnets of E.E. Cummings, which were read at his wedding, or the delicate and moving wordplay of the contemporary Scottish poet Don Paterson.

For singer and songwriter **Cerys Matthews,** internationally renowned for her work with the band Catatonia and as a solo artist, poetry has been vital in celebrating her fiercely proud Welsh identity. Homesick while living in Nashville, she turned to the work of Dylan Thomas and the Welsh bards. From there she developed a love of the greatest Celtic writers, not just of her homeland but also of Ireland and Scotland: W. B. Yeats, Seamus Heaney and Robert Burns.

Writer **Malorie Blackman** was made an OBE in 2008. She is best known for her novels for children and young adults, most notably the award-winning *Noughts & Crosses* sequence, which explores racism and violence from a unique perspective. Growing up in South London, Blackman was introduced to traditional verse at school, but later in her life she discovered the poetry of the multi-cultural streets around her: the Jamaican rhythms of James Berry and Benjamin Zephaniah. Her selections show how poetry has given a voice and an identity to all races and nations.

Life in Verse

Journeys through Poetry

PENGUIN BOOKS

PENGUIN CLASSICS

Published by the Penguin Group
Penguin Books Ltd, 80 Strand, London WC2R ORL, England
Penguin Group (USA) Inc., 375 Hudson Street, New York, New York 10014, USA
Penguin Group (Canada), 90 Eglinton Avenue East, Suite 700, Toronto, Ontario, Canada M4P 2Y3
(a division of Pearson Penguin Canada Inc.)
Penguin Ireland, 25 St Stephen's Green, Dublin 2, Ireland (a division of Penguin Books Ltd)
Penguin Group (Australia), 250 Camberwell Road, Camberwell, Victoria 3124, Australia
(a division of Pearson Australia Group Pty Ltd)
Penguin Books India Pvt Ltd, 11 Community Centre, Panchsheel Park, New Delhi – 110 017, India
Penguin Group (NZ), 67 Apollo Drive, Rosedale, North Shore 0632, New Zealand
(a division of Pearson New Zealand Ltd)
Penguin Books (South Africa) (Pty) Ltd, 24 Sturdee Avenue, Rosebank, Johannesburg 2196, South Africa

Penguin Books Ltd, Registered Offices: 80 Strand, London WC2R ORL, England

www.penguin.com

First published in hardback in Penguin Classics 2009
Published in paperback in Penguin Classics 2010

1

Selection copyright © Penguin Books Ltd, 2009
BBC and the BBC logo are trademarks of the British Broadcasting Corporation and are used under licence.
BBC logo © BBC 1996
The television programme, *My Life in Verse*, is copyright © Wall to Wall Media Ltd

Series producer: Ian MacMillan; executive producers: Lucy Carter, Alex Graham
All rights reserved

The Acknowledgements on pages 254–61 constitute an extension of this copyright page

wall to wall

A Shedmedia® Company

Wall to Wall is one of the world's leading producers of factual and drama content. Now in its 21st year,
the company continues to grow at an unprecedented rate driven by innovative and popular content and
brands which span genres including features, factual entertainment, specialist factual, drama, current
affairs and arts. Wall to Wall has won every major award including a Peabody Award (*1900 House*), an
Emmy (*Baby, It's You*), a host of Broadcast Awards (*Who Do You Think You Are?*) and in 2009 an
Outstanding British Film BAFTA and an Academy Award ® for Best Documentary Feature (*Man on Wire*).
In November 2007 Wall to Wall became part of the Shed Media Group.

Printed in England by Clays Ltd, St Ives plc

ISBN 978-0-140-42481-2

www.greenpenguin.co.uk

Contents

Note on the Selection   xvii

Robert Webb: Modern Life

T. S. ELIOT
   The Love Song of J. Alfred Prufrock   3
   Whispers of Immortality   8
   Journey of the Magi   10
   Rhapsody on a Windy Night   12
   La Figlia Che Piange   15
   Preludes   16

MATTHEW ARNOLD
   The Buried Life   18
   Dover Beach   21

E.E. CUMMINGS
   'i carry your heart with me(i carry it in'   23
   'it may not always be so;and i say'   24
   'one's not half two.   It's two are halves of one:'   25
   'come,gaze with me upon this dome'   26

FELIX DENNIS
   Perfect Day   27
   Poets Anonymous   28

HART CRANE
   Chaplinesque   29

WILLIAM BLAKE
A Dream 30

GERARD MANLEY HOPKINS
'No worst, there is none. Pitched past pitch of grief' 31
'I wake and feel the fell of dark, not day.' 32
'My own heart let me more have pity on' 33

W. H. AUDEN
The Wanderer 34
As I Walked Out One Evening 35
Their Lonely Betters 37
Night Mail 38

THOMAS HARDY
On a Midsummer Eve 40

LOUIS MACNEICE
The Libertine 41

THEODORE ROETHKE
In a Dark Time 42

JOHN BERRYMAN
Dream Song 14 43
Dream Song 312 44

WILLIAM SHAKESPEARE:
'To be, or not to be', from *Hamlet* (Act III, Scene i) 45

ROBERT LOWELL
Skunk Hour 47

ALLEN GINSBERG
'I saw the best minds of my generation destroyed by
madness', from *Howl* 49

RUPERT BROOKE
  The Great Lover   51
  The Old Vicarage, Grantchester   54

PHILIP LARKIN
  The Whitsun Weddings   59
  This Be the Verse   61
  An Arundel Tomb   62
  Friday Night in the Royal Station Hotel 64

DON PATERSON
  '96   65
  The Thread   66

SEAMUS HEANEY
  The Skunk   67
  Casting and Gathering   68

SYLVIA PLATH
  Morning Song   69
  Lady Lazarus   70
  Ariel   74

Cerys Matthews: Britain in Poetry

ANEIRIN
  'Of manly disposition was the youth',
    from Y *Gododdin*   79

DYLAN THOMAS
  The force that through the green fuse   83
  After the funeral   84
  The hunchback in the park   86
  In my craft or sullen art   88
  Fern Hill   89
  Do not go gentle into that good night   91
  And death shall have no dominion   92

IDRIS DAVIES
  The Bells of Rhymney   93

W. B. YEATS
  Down by the Salley Gardens   94
  The Song of Wandering Aengus   95
  The Wild Swans at Coole   96
  Easter, 1916   98
  Under Ben Bulben   101
  The Song of the Happy Shepherd   105
  The Lake Isle of Innisfree   107
  No Second Troy   108
  The Second Coming   109

PATRICK KAVANAGH
  On Raglan Road   110

LOUIS MACNEICE
  Snow   111

SEAMUS HEANEY
  Punishment   112

MICHAEL LONGLEY
  Ceasefire   114
  Wounds   115

NUALA NÍ DHOMHNAILL, TRANSLATED BY
PAUL MULDOON
  The Language Issue   116

CIARAN CARSON
  Belfast Confetti   117

ROBERT BURNS
  Ode to a Haggis   118
  Mary Morison   120
  A Red, Red Rose   121

A Man's a Man for A' That 122
Ae Fond Kiss 124

EDWIN MORGAN
King Billy 125

HUGH MACDIARMID
'The language that but sparely floo'ers',
from *A Drunk Man Looks at the Thistle* 127
Scotland Small? 130

TED HUGHES
The Warriors of the North 131
Heptonstall Old Church 132

C. DAY LEWIS
'You that love England, who have an ear for her
music' 133

Malorie Blackman: Searching for a Voice

WILLIAM BLAKE
London 137
Jerusalem 138
A Poison Tree 139

WILLIAM SHAKESPEARE
'It is the cause, it is the cause', from
Othello (Act V, Scene ii) 140

JOHN MILTON
'Of man's first disobedience, and the fruit',
from *Paradise Lost*: Book I 141
'He ceased, and next him Moloch, sceptred king',
from *Paradise Lost*: Book II 142

EMILY DICKINSON
  'From Cocoon forth a Butterfly'   144
  '"Hope" is the thing with feathers –'   145
  'Good Morning – Midnight –'   146
  ''Tis good – the looking back on Grief –'   147

MAYA ANGELOU
  Still I Rise   148
  Impeccable Conception   150

JAMES BERRY
  In Our Year 1941 My Letter to You Mother Africa   151
  On an Afternoon Train from Purley to
    Victoria, 1955   156

BENJAMIN ZEPHANIAH
  Civil Lies   157
  Walking Black Home   158
  The British   159

GRACE NICHOLS
  Wherever I Hang   161
  Of Course When They Ask for Poems About the
    'Realities' of Black Women   162

JACKIE KAY
  In my country   165
  Her   166

LANGSTON HUGHES
  The Weary Blues   167
  The Negro Speaks of Rivers   168
  Song for a Dark Girl   169
  Harlem Sweeties   170
  Theme for English B   172
  Freedom   174
  Frederick Douglass: 1817–1895   175

ROY CAMPBELL
  The Sisters 176
  Choosing a Mast 177

KONA MACPHEE
  My People 180

OGDEN NASH
  The Cow 181
  Reflections of Ice-breaking 181
  Requiem 182
  The Turtle 182
  Arthur 182

LEWIS CARROLL
  Jabberwocky 183
  The Mad Gardener's Song 185

ROALD DAHL
  'I've Eaten Many Strange and Scrumptious
    Dishes . . .' 187

EDWARD GOREY
  There's a Rather Odd Couple in Herts 189
  From Number Nine, Penwiper Mews 189

A. E. HOUSMAN
  The Elephant or, The Force of Habit 190
  from The Crocodile or, Public Decency 191

EDWARD LEAR
  The Owl and the Pussy-Cat 193

RICHARD EDWARDS
  Stevie Scared 194

HILAIRE BELLOC
  Matilda (Who Told Lies, and Was Burned to Death) 195

Sheila Hancock: Love and Loss

RAYMOND CARVER
Late Fragment   199

WILLIAM CARLOS WILLIAMS
The Ivy Crown   200

W. H. AUDEN
Lullaby   203
Stop All the Clocks   204

GEORGE HERBERT
Love (III)   205

ARTHUR HUGH CLOUGH
Put Forth Thy Leaf   206
Not in Vain   207

DANTE GABRIEL ROSSETTI
The One Hope   208

ELIZABETH BARRETT BROWNING
Loved Once   209
Comfort   211
Irreparableness   212
Sonnets from the Portuguese XLIII   213
Grief   214

CHRISTOPHER P. CRANCH
Enosis   215

WILLIAM WORDSWORTH
Desideria   216

ADAM ZAGAJEWSKI
Try to Praise the Mutilated World   217

MATTHEW ARNOLD
   Growing Old   218

EDNA ST VINCENT MILLAY
   'As to some lovely temple, tenantless'   219
   'Time does not bring relief; you all have lied'   220
   Dirge Without Music   221

W. B. YEATS
   When You Are Old   222

ROBERT FROST
   The Oven Bird   223

PHILIP LARKIN
   Mother, Summer, I   224
   The Mower   225

ALFRED, LORD TENNYSON
   Break, Break, Break   226

BRIAN PATTEN
   So Many Different Lengths of Time   227

JOHN MILTON
   'When I consider how my light is spent'   229

PERCY BYSSHE SHELLEY
   Love's Philosophy   230

WALTER DE LA MARE
   The Listeners   231

RUDYARD KIPLING
   The Way through the Woods   233

WILLIAM SHAKESPEARE
    'Howl, howl, howl! O, you are men of stones!',
      from *King Lear* (Act V, Scene iii)   234

SAINT FRANCIS OF ASSISI
    'Lord, make me an instrument of your peace.'   235

EMILY BRONTË
    'No coward soul is mine'   236

PRIMO LEVI
    To My Friends   237

STEVIE SMITH
    Not Waving But Drowning   238
    Pad, pad   238

JOHN KEATS
    To Autumn   239

CHRISTINA ROSSETTI
    Remember   240

W. H. DAVIES
    Leisure   241

WILLIAM BLAKE
    The Sick Rose   242

WILLIAM SHAKESPEARE
    Sonnet 29   243
    Sonnet 30   244
    Sonnet 73   245

WILLIAM HALL
    'Where ducks by scores travers'd the fens',
      from *Memories of a Decoy*   246

EMILY DICKINSON
   'I'm Nobody! Who are you?'   246
   'After great pain, a formal feeling comes –'   247

ALFRED, LORD TENNYSON
   'Dark house, by which once more I stand',
      from *In Memoriam A. H. H.*   248

LOUIS MACNEICE
   The Sunlight on the Garden   249

HENRY VAUGHAN
   Man   250

WALT WHITMAN
   'An old man bending', from 'The Wound Dresser'   252
   I Saw in Louisiana a Live-Oak Growing   253

   Acknowledgements   254
   Index of Titles and First Lines   262

Note on the Selection

In spring 2009, the BBC showed a four-part television series called *My Life in Verse*. Reading many of the poems aloud and directly to camera, Robert Webb, Cerys Matthews, Malorie Blackman and Sheila Hancock discussed some of their favourite poems and the role that poetry has played and continues to play in their lives. The aim of the series was to show how poetry, even poetry written hundreds of years ago, can come to life in its encounter with individual experience.

The poems in this volume were selected to accompany and enhance those discussed by Robert Webb, Cerys Matthews, Malorie Blackman and Sheila Hancock in the television series. In each case, the presenter's selection of poems from the programme suggested a theme to me, which I supplemented further with poems complementary in tone and theme. Robert Webb's section is 'Modern Life' and the voice of modern bewilderment in T. S. Eliot's 'The Love Song of J. Alfred Prufrock' is set alongside equally distraught or bemused voices in poems by other authors including Shakespeare, Gerard Manley Hopkins and John Berryman. Cerys Matthews's choices express not only her love of Wales, Ireland and Scotland, but also her sensitivity to the music of poetry. Malorie Blackman's journey through poetry is closely connected to her search for a voice and an identity of her own. Beginning at school with canonical poets such as Milton, she later found that her voice more fully resounded in black British and American poets, such as Benjamin Zephaniah, and finally in the children's and nonsense verse of poets such as Edward Lear. Her section, more than any other, is full of diverse voices. And finally, the actress Sheila

Hancock's section is devoted to the poems of love and grief that consoled her after the death of her husband. To the work of poets such as Tennyson, Blake and Larkin were added poems by Shakespeare, Emily Dickinson and Edna St Vincent Millay, amongst others.

Alexis Kirschbaum
Penguin Classics

ROBERT WEBB

Modern Life

'Let us go then, you and I'

T.S. Eliot, 'The Love Song
of J. Alfred Prufrock'

T. S. ELIOT

The Love Song of J. Alfred Prufrock

S'io credessi che mia risposta fosse
a persona che mai tornasse al mondo,
questa fiamma staria senza più scosse.
Ma per ciò che giammai di questo fondo
non tornò vivo alcun, s'i'odo il vero,
senza tema d'infamia ti rispondo.

Let us go then, you and I,
When the evening is spread out against the sky
Like a patient etherised upon a table;
Let us go, through certain half-deserted streets,
The muttering retreats
Of restless nights in one-night cheap hotels
And sawdust restaurants with oyster-shells:
Streets that follow like a tedious argument
Of insidious intent
To lead you to an overwhelming question . . .
Oh, do not ask, 'What is it?'
Let us go and make our visit.

In the room the women come and go
Talking of Michelangelo.

The yellow fog that rubs its back upon the window-panes,
The yellow smoke that rubs its muzzle on the
          window-panes,
Licked its tongue into the corners of the evening,
Lingered upon the pools that stand in drains,
Let fall upon its back the soot that falls from chimneys,
Slipped by the terrace, made a sudden leap,
And seeing that it was a soft October night,
Curled once about the house, and fell asleep.

And indeed there will be time
For the yellow smoke that slides along the street
Rubbing its back upon the window-panes;
There will be time, there will be time
To prepare a face to meet the faces that you meet;
There will be time to murder and create,
And time for all the works and days of hands
That lift and drop a question on your plate;
Time for you and time for me,
And time yet for a hundred indecisions,
And for a hundred visions and revisions,
Before the taking of a toast and tea.

In the room the women come and go
Talking of Michelangelo.

And indeed there will be time
To wonder, 'Do I dare?' and, 'Do I dare?'
Time to turn back and descend the stair,
With a bald spot in the middle of my hair—
(They will say: 'How his hair is growing thin!')
My morning coat, my collar mounting firmly to the chin,
My necktie rich and modest, but asserted by a simple pin—
(They will say: 'But how his arms and legs are thin!')
Do I dare
Disturb the universe?
In a minute there is time
For decisions and revisions which a minute will reverse.

For I have known them all already, known them all—
Have known the evenings, mornings, afternoons,
I have measured out my life with coffee spoons;
I know the voices dying with a dying fall
Beneath the music from a farther room.
    So how should I presume?

And I have known the eyes already, known them all—
The eyes that fix you in a formulated phrase,

And when I am formulated, sprawling on a pin,
When I am pinned and wriggling on the wall,
Then how should I begin
To spit out all the butt-ends of my days and ways?
    And how should I presume?

And I have known the arms already, known them all—
Arms that are braceleted and white and bare
(But in the lamplight, downed with light brown hair!)
Is it perfume from a dress
That makes me so digress?
Arms that lie along a table, or wrap about a shawl.
    And should I then presume?
    And how should I begin?

    • • • • •

Shall I say, I have gone at dusk through narrow streets
And watched the smoke that rises from the pipes
Of lonely men in shirt-sleeves, leaning out of windows? . . .

I should have been a pair of ragged claws
Scuttling across the floors of silent seas.

    • • • • •

And the afternoon, the evening, sleeps so peacefully!
Smoothed by long fingers,
Asleep . . . tired . . . or it malingers,
Stretched on the floor, here beside you and me.
Should I, after tea and cakes and ices,
Have the strength to force the moment to its crisis?
But though I have wept and fasted, wept and prayed,
Though I have seen my head (grown slightly bald)
       brought in upon a platter,
I am no prophet—and here's no great matter;
I have seen the moment of my greatness flicker,
And I have seen the eternal Footman hold my coat, and
       snicker,
And in short, I was afraid.

And would it have been worth it, after all,
After the cups, the marmalade, the tea,
Among the porcelain, among some talk of you and me,
Would it have been worth while,
To have bitten off the matter with a smile,
To have squeezed the universe into a ball
To roll it towards some overwhelming question,
To say: 'I am Lazarus, come from the dead,
Come back to tell you all, I shall tell you all'—
If one, settling a pillow by her head,
    Should say: 'That is not what I meant at all.
    That is not it, at all.'

And would it have been worth it, after all,
Would it have been worth while,
After the sunsets and the dooryards and the sprinkled
        streets,
After the novels, after the teacups, after the skirts that
        trail along the floor—
And this, and so much more?—
It is impossible to say just what I mean!
But as if a magic lantern threw the nerves in patterns on a
        screen:
Would it have been worth while
If one, settling a pillow or throwing off a shawl,
And turning toward the window, should say:
    'That is not it at all,
    That is not what I meant, at all.'

            •   •   •   •   •

No! I am not Prince Hamlet, nor was meant to be;
Am an attendant lord, one that will do
To swell a progress, start a scene or two,
Advise the prince; no doubt, an easy tool,
Deferential, glad to be of use,
Politic, cautious, and meticulous;
Full of high sentence, but a bit obtuse;
At times, indeed, almost ridiculous—
Almost, at times, the Fool.

I grow old . . . I grow old . . .
I shall wear the bottoms of my trousers rolled.

Shall I part my hair behind? Do I dare to eat a peach?
I shall wear white flannel trousers, and walk upon the
     beach.
I have heard the mermaids singing, each to each.

I do not think that they will sing to me.

I have seen them riding seaward on the waves
Combing the white hair of the waves blown back
When the wind blows the water white and black.

We have lingered in the chambers of the sea
By sea-girls wreathed with seaweed red and brown
Till human voices wake us, and we drown.

T. S. ELIOT

Whispers of Immortality

Webster was much possessed by death
And saw the skull beneath the skin;
And breastless creatures under ground
Leaned backward with a lipless grin.

Daffodil bulbs instead of balls
Stared from the sockets of the eyes!
He knew that thought clings round dead limbs
Tightening its lusts and luxuries.

Donne, I suppose, was such another
Who found no substitute for sense,
To seize and clutch and penetrate;
Expert beyond experience,

He knew the anguish of the marrow
The ague of the skeleton;
No contact possible to flesh
Allayed the fever of the bone.

· · · · ·

Grishkin is nice: her Russian eye
Is underlined for emphasis;
Uncorseted, her friendly bust
Gives promise of pneumatic bliss.

The couched Brazilian jaguar
Compels the scampering marmoset
With subtle effluence of cat;
Grishkin has a maisonnette;

The sleek Brazilian jaguar
Does not in its arboreal gloom
Distil so rank a feline smell
As Grishkin in a drawing-room.

And even the Abstract Entities
Circumambulate her charm;
But our lot crawls between dry ribs
To keep our metaphysics warm.

T. S. ELIOT

Journey of the Magi

'A cold coming we had of it.
Just the worst time of the year
For a journey, and such a long journey:
The ways deep and the weather sharp,
The very dead of winter.'
And the camels galled, sore-footed, refractory,
Lying down in the melting snow.
There were times we regretted
The summer palaces on slopes, the terraces.
And the silken girls bringing sherbet.

Then the camel men cursing and grumbling
And running away, and wanting their liquor and
      women,
And the night-fires going out, and the lack of shelters,
And the cities hostile and the towns unfriendly
And the villages dirty and charging high prices:
A hard time we had of it.
At the end we preferred to travel all night,
Sleeping in snatches,
With the voices singing in our ears, saying
That this was all folly.

Then at dawn we came down to a temperate valley,
Wet, below the snow line, smelling of vegetation,
With a running stream and a water-mill beating the
      darkness,
And three trees on the low sky.
And an old white horse galloped away in the meadow.
Then we came to a tavern with vine-leaves over the
      lintel,

Six hands at an open door dicing for pieces of silver,
And feet kicking the empty wine-skins.
But there was no information, and so we continued
And arrived at evening, not a moment too soon
Finding the place; it was (you may say) satisfactory.

　　All this was a long time ago, I remember,
And I would do it again, but set down
This set down
This: were we led all that way for
Birth or Death? There was a Birth, certainly,
We had evidence and no doubt. I had seen birth and
　　　　death,
But had thought they were different; this Birth was
Hard and bitter agony for us, like Death, our death.
We returned to our places, these Kingdoms,
But no longer at ease here, in the old dispensation,
With an alien people clutching their gods.
I should be glad of another death.

T. S. ELIOT

Rhapsody on a Windy Night

Twelve o'clock.
Along the reaches of the street
Held in a lunar synthesis,
Whispering lunar incantations
Dissolve the floors of memory
And all its clear relations,
Its divisions and precisions,
Every street lamp that I pass
Beats like a fatalistic drum,
And through the spaces of the dark
Midnight shakes the memory
As a madman shakes a dead geranium.

Half-past one,
The street lamp sputtered,
The street lamp muttered,
The street lamp said, 'Regard that woman
Who hesitates towards you in the light of the door
Which opens on her like a grin.
You see the border of her dress
Is torn and stained with sand,
And you see the corner of her eye
Twists like a crooked pin.'

The memory throws up high and dry
A crowd of twisted things;
A twisted branch upon the beach
Eaten smooth, and polished
As if the world gave up
The secret of its skeleton,
Stiff and white.

A broken spring in a factory yard,
Rust that clings to the form that the strength has left
Hard and curled and ready to snap.

Half-past two,
The street lamp said,
'Remark the cat which flattens itself in the gutter,
Slips out its tongue
And devours a morsel of rancid butter.'
So the hand of a child, automatic,
Slipped out and pocketed a toy that was running
    along the quay.
I could see nothing behind that child's eye.
I have seen eyes in the street
Trying to peer through lighted shutters,
And a crab one afternoon in a pool,
An old crab with barnacles on his back,
Gripped the end of a stick which I held him.

Half-past three,
The lamp sputtered,
The lamp muttered in the dark.

The lamp hummed:
'Regard the moon,
La lune ne garde aucune rancune,
She winks a feeble eye,
She smiles into corners.
She smoothes the hair of the grass.
The moon has lost her memory.
A washed-out smallpox cracks her face,
Her hand twists a paper rose,
That smells of dust and old Cologne,
She is alone
With all the old nocturnal smells
That cross and cross across her brain.'
The reminiscence comes
Of sunless dry geraniums

And dust in crevices,
Smells of chestnuts in the streets,
And female smells in shuttered rooms,
And cigarettes in corridors
And cocktail smells in bars.

The lamp said,
'Four o'clock,
Here is the number on the door.
Memory!
You have the key,
The little lamp spreads a ring on the stair,
Mount.
The bed is open; the tooth-brush hangs on the wall,
Put your shoes at the door, sleep, prepare for life.'

The last twist of the knife.

La Figlia Che Piange

O quam te memorem virgo –

Stand on the highest pavement of the stair –
Lean on a garden urn –
Weave, weave the sunlight in your hair –
Clasp your flowers to you with a pained surprise –
Fling them to the ground and turn
With a fugitive resentment in your eyes:
But weave, weave the sunlight in your hair.

So I would have had him leave,
So I would have had her stand and grieve,
So he would have left
As the soul leaves the body torn and bruised,
As the mind deserts the body it has used.
I should find
Some way incomparably light and deft,
Some way we both should understand,
Simple and faithless as a smile and shake of the hand.

She turned away, but with the autumn weather
Compelled my imagination many days,
Many days and many hours:
Her hair over her arms and her arms full of flowers.
And I wonder how they should have been together!
I should have lost a gesture and a pose.
Sometimes these cogitations still amaze
The troubled midnight and the noon's repose.

T. S. ELIOT

Preludes

The winter evening settles down
With smell of steaks in passageways.
Six o'clock.
The burnt-out ends of smoky days.
And now a gusty shower wraps
The grimy scraps
Of withered leaves about your feet
And newspapers from vacant lots;
The showers beat
On broken blinds and chimney-pots,
And at the corner of the street
A lonely cab-horse steams and stamps.

And then the lighting of the lamps.

II

The morning comes to consciousness
Of faint stale smells of beer
From the sawdust-trampled street
With all its muddy feet that press
To early coffee-stands.

With the other masquerades
That time resumes,
One thinks of all the hands
That are raising dingy shades
In a thousand furnished rooms.

III

You tossed a blanket from the bed,
You lay upon your back, and waited;
You dozed, and watched the night revealing
The thousand sordid images
Of which your soul was constituted;
They flickered against the ceiling.
And when all the world came back
And the light crept up between the shutters,
And you heard the sparrows in the gutters,
You had such a vision of the street
As the street hardly understands;
Sitting along the bed's edge, where
You curled the papers from your hair,
Or clasped the yellow soles of feet
In the palms of both soiled hands.

IV

His soul stretched tight across the skies
That fade behind a city block,
Or trampled by insistent feet
At four and five and six o'clock;
And short square fingers stuffing pipes,
And evening newspapers, and eyes
Assured of certain certainties,
The conscience of a blackened street
Impatient to assume the world.

I am moved by fancies that are curled
Around these images, and cling:
The notion of some infinitely gentle
Infinitely suffering thing.

Wipe your hand across your mouth, and laugh;
The worlds revolve like ancient women
Gathering fuel in vacant lots.

MATTHEW ARNOLD

The Buried Life

Light flows our war of mocking words, and yet,
Behold, with tears mine eyes are wet!
I feel a nameless sadness o'er me roll.
Yes, yes, we know that we can jest,
We know, we know that we can smile!
But there's a something in this breast,
To which thy light words bring no rest,
And thy gay smiles no anodyne.
Give me thy hand, and hush awhile,
And turn those limpid eyes on mine,
And let me read there, love! thy inmost soul.

Alas! is even love too weak
To unlock the heart, and let it speak?
Are even lovers powerless to reveal
To one another what indeed they feel?
I knew the mass of men conceal'd
Their thoughts, for fear that if reveal'd
They would by other men be met
With blank indifference, or with blame reproved;
I knew they lived and moved
Trick'd in disguises, alien to the rest
Of men, and alien to themselves—and yet
The same heart beats in every human breast!

But we, my love!—doth a like spell benumb
Our hearts, our voices?—must we too be dumb?

Ah! well for us, if even we,
Even for a moment, can get free
Our heart, and have our lips unchain'd;
For that which seals them hath been deep-ordain'd!

Fate, which foresaw
How frivolous a baby man would be—
By what distractions he would be possess'd,
How he would pour himself in every strife,
And well-nigh change his own identity—
That it might keep from his capricious play
His genuine self, and force him to obey
Even in his own despite his being's law,
Bade through the deep recesses of our breast
The unregarded river of our life
Pursue with indiscernible flow its way;
And that we should not see
The buried stream, and seem to be
Eddying at large in blind uncertainty,
Though driving on with it eternally.

But often, in the world's most crowded streets,
But often, in the din of strife,
There rises an unspeakable desire
After the knowledge of our buried life;
A thirst to spend our fire and restless force
In tracking out our true, original course;
A longing to inquire
Into the mystery of this heart which beats
So wild, so deep in us—to know
Whence our lives come and where they go.
And many a man in his own breast then delves,
But deep enough, alas! none ever mines.
And we have been on many thousand lines,
And we have shown, on each, spirit and power;
But hardly have we, for one little hour,
Been on our own line, have we been ourselves—
Hardly had skill to utter one of all
The nameless feelings that course through our
    breast,
But they course on for ever unexpress'd.
And long we try in vain to speak and act

Our hidden self, and what we say and do
Is eloquent, is well—but 'tis not true!
And then we will no more be rack'd
With inward striving, and demand
Of all the thousand nothings of the hour
Their stupefying power;
Ah yes, and they benumb us at our call!
Yet still, from time to time, vague and forlorn,
From the soul's subterranean depth upborne
As from an infinitely distant land,
Come airs, and floating echoes, and convey
A melancholy into all our day.

Only—but this is rare—
When a beloved hand is laid in ours,
When, jaded with the rush and glare
Of the interminable hours,
Our eyes can in another's eyes read clear,
When our world-deafen'd ear
Is by the tones of a loved voice caress'd—
A bolt is shot back somewhere in our breast,
And a lost pulse of feeling stirs again.
The eye sinks inward, and the heart lies plain,
And what we mean, we say, and what we would, we
    know.
A man becomes aware of his life's flow,
And hears its winding murmur; and he sees
The meadows where it glides, the sun, the breeze.

And there arrives a lull in the hot race
Wherein he doth for ever chase
That flying and elusive shadow, rest.
An air of coolness plays upon his face,
And an unwonted calm pervades his breast.
And then he thinks he knows
The hills where his life rose,
And the sea where it goes.

Dover Beach

The sea is calm to-night.
The tide is full, the moon lies fair
Upon the straits; – on the French coast the light
Gleams and is gone; the cliffs of England stand,
Glimmering and vast, out in the tranquil bay.
Come to the window, sweet is the night-air!
Only, from the long line of spray
Where the sea meets the moon-blanch'd land,
Listen! you hear the grating roar
Of pebbles which the waves draw back, and fling,
At their return, up the high strand,
Begin, and cease, and then again begin,
With tremulous cadence slow, and bring
The eternal note of sadness in.

Sophocles long ago
Heard it on the Aegean, and it brought
Into his mind the turbid ebb and flow
Of human misery; we
Find also in the sound a thought,
Hearing it by this distant northern sea.

The Sea of Faith
Was once, too, at the full, and round earth's shore
Lay like the folds of a bright girdle furl'd.
But now I only hear
Its melancholy, long, withdrawing roar,
Retreating, to the breath
Of the night-wind, down the vast edges drear
And naked shingles of the world.

Ah, love, let us be true
To one another! for the world, which seems
To lie before us like a land of dreams,
So various, so beautiful, so new,
Hath really neither joy, nor love, nor light,
Nor certitude, nor peace, nor help for pain;
And we are here as on a darkling plain
Swept with confused alarms of struggle and flight,
Where ignorant armies clash by night.

E.E. CUMMINGS

'i carry your heart with me(i carry it in'

i carry your heart with me(i carry it in
my heart)i am never without it(anywhere
i go you go, my dear;and whatever is done
by only me is your doing,my darling)
                                    i fear
no fate(for you are my fate,my sweet)i want
no world(for beautiful you are my world,my true)
and it's you are whatever a moon has always meant
and whatever a sun will always sing is you

here is the deepest secret nobody knows
(here is the root of the root and the bud of the bud
and the sky of the sky of a tree called life;which grows
higher than soul can hope or mind can hide)
and this is the wonder that's keeping the stars apart

i carry your heart(i carry it in my heart)

E.E. CUMMINGS

'it may not always be so;and i say'

it may not always be so;and i say
that if your lips,which i have loved,should touch
another's,and your dear strong fingers clutch
his heart,as mine in time not far away;
if on another's face your sweet hair lay
in such a silence as i know,or such
great writhing words as,uttering overmuch,
stand helplessly before the spirit at bay;

if this should be,i say if this should be—
you of my heart, send me a little word;
that i may go unto him,and take his hands,
saying,Accept all happiness from me.
Then shall i turn my face,and hear one bird
sing terribly afar in the lost lands.

E.E. CUMMINGS

'one's not half two.   It's two
are halves of one:'

one's not half two.   It's two are halves of one:
which halves reintegrating,shall occur
no death and any quantity;but than
all numerable mosts the actual more

minds ignorant of stern miraculous
this every truth—beware of heartless them
(given the scalpel,they dissect a kiss;
or,sold the reason,they undream a dream)

one is the song which fiends and angels sing:
all murdering lies by mortals told make two.
Let liars wilt,repaying life they're loaned;
we(by a gift called dying born)must grow

deep in dark least ourselves remembering
love only rides his year.
                                        All lose,whole find

E.E. CUMMINGS

'come,gaze with me upon this dome'

come,gaze with me upon this dome
of many coloured glass,and see
his mother's pride,his father's joy,
unto whom duty whispers low

"thou must!" and who replies "I can!"
—yon clean upstanding well dressed boy
that with his peers full oft hath quaffed
the wine of life and found it sweet—

a tear within his stern blue eye,
upon his firm white lips a smile,
one thought alone:to do or die
for God for country and for Yale

above his blond determined head
the sacred flag of truth unfurled,
in the bright heyday of his youth
the upper class American

unsullied stands,before the world:
with manly heart and conscience free,
upon the front steps of her home
by the high minded pure young girl

much kissed,by loving relatives
well fed,and fully photographed
the son of man goes forth to war
with trumpets clap and syphilis

FELIX DENNIS

Perfect Day

Today was one of the best days of my life.
Nothing of any importance occurred —
I cut my finger on a paperknife
And marvelled at a busy hummingbird
Plucking out wet moss by a waterfall;
Broke bread with friends and shared a glass of wine;
Wrote this poem; swam; made love. That's all.
Why should it be some days erect a shrine,
A cairn, a white stone day, in memory?
Is it, as Buddhists claim, a lack of need,
Or want — or simple serendipity —
The perfect flowering of one small seed?
    The wise will say our frames are none too pure:
    How many perfect days could we endure?

FELIX DENNIS

Poets Anonymous

'My name is Felix and I am a poet.
I became a poet five years ago
Following an illness. Of course, that's no
Excuse—the illness, I mean. I know.

We know about the world poets inhabit—
The wreckage their behaviour brings to wives,
Husbands, children, etc. How the habit
Sours and decimates our loved-ones' lives,

Eating up time we could be spending
Late at the office, earning a crust
To pay for our children's mobile phone bills.
Or watching TV with the family. We must

Be honest with ourselves. Think of the horrible
Embarrassment of a loved one forced to say:
"Well, to be honest, he/she is a poet."
The appalled silence as they turn away.

We know all that. How we break promises
To take up stamp collecting. We know it,
Locked away in our own little selfish world.
My name is Felix and I am a poet.'

HART CRANE

Chaplinesque

We make our meek adjustments,
Contented with such random consolations
As the wind deposits
In slithered and too ample pockets.

For we can still love the world, who find
A famished kitten on the step, and know
Recesses for it from the fury of the street,
Or warm torn elbow coverts.

We will sidestep, and to the final smirk
Dally the doom of that inevitable thumb
That slowly chafes its puckered index toward us,
Facing the dull squint with what innocence
And what surprise!

And yet these fine collapses are not lies
More than the pirouettes of any pliant cane;
Our obsequies are, in a way, no enterprise.
We can evade you, and all else but the heart:
What blame to us if the heart live on.

The game enforces smirks; but we have seen
The moon in lonely alleys make
A grail of laughter of an empty ash can,
And through all sound of gaiety and quest
Have heard a kitten in the wilderness.

WILLIAM BLAKE

A Dream

Once a dream did weave a shade,
O'er my Angel-guarded bed,
That an Emmet lost it's way
Where on grass methought I lay.

Troubled wilderd and folorn
Dark benighted travel-worn,
Over many a tangled spray
All heart-broke I heard her say.

O my children! do they cry
Do they hear their father sigh.
Now they look abroad to see,
Now return and weep for me.

Pitying I drop'd a tear:
But I saw a glow-worm near:
Who replied. What wailing wight
Calls the watchman of the night.

I am set to light the ground,
While the beetle goes his round:
Follow now the beetles hum,
Little wanderer hie thee home.

GERARD MANLEY HOPKINS

'No *worst, there is none. Pitched past pitch of grief*'

No worst, there is none. Pitched past pitch of grief,
More pangs will, schooled at forepangs, wilder wring.
Comforter, where, where is your comforting?
Mary, mother of us, where is your relief?

My cries heave, herds-long; huddle in a main, a chief-
woe, world-sorrow; on an age-old anvil wince and sing—
Then lull, then leave off. Fury had shrieked "No ling-
ering! Let me be fell: force I must be brief".

O the mind, mind has mountains; cliffs of fall
Frightful, sheer, no-man-fathomed. Hold them cheap
May who ne'er hung there. Nor does long our small
Durance deal with that steep or deep. Here! creep,
Wretch, under a comfort serves in a whirlwind: all
Life death does end and each day dies with sleep.

GERARD MANLEY HOPKINS

'I wake and feel the fell of dark, not day.'

I wake and feel the fell of dark, not day.
What hours, O what black hoürs we have spent
This night! what sights you, heart, saw; ways you went!
And more must, in yet longer light's delay.

With witness I speak this. But where I say
Hours I mean years, mean life. And my lament
Is cries countless, cries like dead letters sent
To dearest him that lives alas! away.

I am gall, I am heartburn. God's most deep decree
Bitter would have me taste: my taste was me;
Bones built in me, flesh filled, blood brimmed the curse.

Selfyeast of spirit a dull dough sours. I see
The lost are like this, and their scourge to be
As I am mine, their sweating selves, but worse.

'My own heart let me more have pity on'

My own heart let me more have pity on; let
Me live to my sad self hereafter kind,
Charitable; not live this tormented mind
With this tormented mind tormenting yet.

I cast for comfort I can no more get
By groping round my comfortless, than blind
Eyes in their dark can day or thirst can find
Thirst's all-in-all in all a world of wet.

Soul, self; come, poor Jackself, I do advise
You, jaded, let be; call off thoughts awhile
Elsewhere; leave comfort root-room; let joy size

At God knows when to God knows what; whose smile
's not wrung, see you; unforeseen times rather—as skies
Betweenpie mountains—lights a lovely mile.

W. H. AUDEN

The Wanderer

Doom is dark and deeper than any sea-dingle.
Upon what man it fall
In spring, day-wishing flowers appearing,
Avalanche sliding, white snow from rock-face,
That he should leave his house,
No cloud-soft hand can hold him, restraint by women;
But ever that man goes
Through place-keepers, through forest trees,
A stranger to strangers over undried sea,
Houses for fishes, suffocating water,
Or lonely on fell as chat,
By pot-holed becks
A bird stone-haunting, an unquiet bird.

There head falls forward, fatigued at evening,
And dreams of home,
Waving from window, spread of welcome,
Kissing of wife under single sheet;
But waking sees
Bird-flocks nameless to him, through doorway voices
Of new men making another love.

Save him from hostile capture,
From sudden tiger's leap at corner;
Protect his house,
His anxious house where days are counted
From thunderbolt protect,
From gradual ruin spreading like a stain;
Converting number from vague to certain,
Bring joy, bring day of his returning,
Lucky with day approaching, with leaning dawn.

W. H. AUDEN

As I Walked Out One Evening

As I walked out one evening,
   Walking down Bristol Street,
The crowds upon the pavement
   Were fields of harvest wheat.

And down by the brimming river
   I heard a lover sing
Under an arch of the railway:
   "Love has no ending.

"I'll love you, dear, I'll love you
   Till China and Africa meet,
And the river jumps over the mountain
   And the salmon sing in the street,

"I'll love you till the ocean
   Is folded and hung up to dry
And the seven stars go squawking
   Like geese about the sky.

"The years shall run like rabbits,
   For in my arms I hold
The Flower of the Ages,
   And the first love of the world."

But all the clocks in the city
   Began to whirr and chime:
"O let not Time deceive you,
   You cannot conquer Time.

"In the burrows of the Nightmare
   Where Justice naked is,
Time watches from the shadow
   And coughs when you would kiss.

"In headaches and in worry
   Vaguely life leaks away.
And Time will have his fancy
   To-morrow or to-day.

"Into many a green valley
   Drifts the appalling snow;
Time breaks the threaded dances
   And the diver's brilliant bow.

"O plunge your hands in water,
   Plunge them in up to the wrist;
Stare, stare in the basin
   And wonder what you've missed.

"The glacier knocks in the cupboard,
   The desert sighs in the bed,
And the crack in the tea-cup opens
   A lane to the land of the dead.

"Where the beggars raffle the banknotes
   And the Giant is enchanting to Jack,
And the Lily-white Boy is a Roarer,
   And Jill goes down on her back.

"O look, look in the mirror,
   O look in your distress;
Life remains a blessing
   Although you cannot bless.

"O stand, stand at the window
    As the tears scald and start;
You shall love your crooked neighbour
    With your crooked heart."

It was late, late in the evening,
    The lovers they were gone;
The clocks had ceased their chiming,
    And the deep river ran on.

W. H. AUDEN

Their Lonely Betters

As I listened from a beach-chair in the shade
To all the noises that my garden made,
It seemed to me only proper that words
Should be withheld from vegetables and birds.

A robin with no Christian name ran through
The Robin-Anthem which was all it knew,
And rustling flowers for some third party waited
To say which pairs, if any, should get mated.

Not one of them was capable of lying,
There was not one which knew that it was dying
Or could have with a rhythm or a rhyme
Assumed responsibility for time.

Let them leave language to their lonely betters
Who count some days and long for certain letters:
We, too, make noises when we laugh or weep:
Words are for those with promises to keep.

W. H. AUDEN

Night Mail

(*Commentary for a G.P.O. Film*)

I

This is the Night Mail crossing the Border,
Bringing the cheque and the postal order,

Letters for the rich, letters for the poor,
The shop at the corner, the girl next door.

Pulling up Beattock, a steady climb:
The gradient's against her, but she's on time.

Past cotton-grass and moorland boulder,
Shovelling white steam over her shoulder,

Snorting noisily, she passes
Silent miles of wind-bent grasses.

Birds turn their heads as she approaches,
Stare from bushes at her blank-faced coaches.

Sheep-dogs cannot turn her course;
They slumber on with paws across.

In the farm she passes no one wakes,
But a jug in a bedroom gently shakes.

II

Dawn freshens. Her climb is done.
Down towards Glasgow she descends,
Towards the steam tugs yelping down a glade of
    cranes,

Towards the fields of apparatus, the furnaces
Set on the dark plain like gigantic chessmen.
All Scotland waits for her:
In dark glens, beside pale-green lochs,
Men long for news.

III

Letters of thanks, letters from banks,
Letters of joy from girl and boy,
Receipted bills and invitations
To inspect new stock or to visit relations,
And applications for situations,
And timid lovers' declarations,
And gossip, gossip from all the nations,
News circumstantial, news financial,
Letters with holiday snaps to enlarge in,
Letters with faces scrawled on the margin,
Letters from uncles, cousins and aunts,
Letters to Scotland from the South of France,
Letters of condolence to Highlands and Lowlands,
Written on paper of every hue,
The pink, the violet, the white and the blue,
The chatty, the catty, the boring, the adoring,
The cold and official and the heart's outpouring,
Clever, stupid, short and long,
The typed and the printed and the spelt all wrong.

IV

Thousands are still asleep,
Dreaming of terrifying monsters
Or a friendly tea beside the band in Cranston's or
    Crawford's:
Asleep in working Glasgow, asleep in well-set
    Edinburgh,
Asleep in granite Aberdeen,
They continue their dreams,
But shall wake soon and hope for letters,

And none will hear the postman's knock
Without a quickening of the heart.
For who can bear to feel himself forgotten?

THOMAS HARDY

On a Midsummer Eve

I idly cut a parsley stalk,
And blew therein towards the moon;
I had not thought what ghosts would walk
With shivering footsteps to my tune.

I went, and knelt, and scooped my hand
As if to drink, into the brook,
And a faint figure seemed to stand
Above me, with the bygone look.

I lipped rough rhymes of chance, not choice,
I thought not what my words might be;
There came into my ear a voice
That turned a tenderer verse for me.

LOUIS MACNEICE

The Libertine

In the old days with married women's stockings
Twisted round his bedpost he felt himself a gay
Dog but now his liver has begun to groan,
Now that pick-ups are the order of the day:
O leave me easy, leave me alone.

Voluptuary in his 'teens and cynic in his twenties,
He ran through women like a child through growing hay
Looking for a lost toy whose capture might atone
For his own guilt and the cosmic disarray:
O leave me easy, leave me alone.

He never found the toy and has forgotten the faces,
Only remembers the props . . . a scent-spray
Beside the bed or a milk-white telephone
Or through the triple ninon the acrid trickle of day:
O leave me easy, leave me alone.

Long fingers over the gunwale, hair in a hair-net,
Furs in January, cartwheel hats in May,
And after the event the wish to be alone—
Angels, goddesses, bitches, all have edged away:
O leave me easy, leave me alone.

So now, in middle age, his erotic programme
Torn in two, if after such a delay
An accident should offer him his own
Fulfilment in a woman, still he would say:
O leave me easy, leave me alone.

THEODORE ROETHKE
In a Dark Time

In a dark time, the eye begins to see,
I meet my shadow in the deepening shade;
I hear my echo in the echoing wood—
A lord of nature weeping to a tree.
I live between the heron and the wren,
Beasts of the hill and serpents of the den.

What's madness but nobility of soul
At odds with circumstances? The day's on fire!
I know the purity of pure despair,
My shadow pinned against a sweating wall.
That place among the rocks—is it a cave,
Or winding path? The edge is what I have.

A steady storm of correspondences!
A night flowing with birds, a ragged moon,
And in broad day the midnight come again!
A man goes far to find out what he is—
Death of the self in a long, tearless night,
All natural shapes blazing unnatural light.

Dark, dark my light, and darker my desire.
My soul, like some heat-maddened summer fly,
Keeps buzzing at the sill. Which I is *I*?
A fallen man, I climb out of my fear.
The mind enters itself, and God the mind,
And one is One, free in the tearing wind.

Dream Song 14

Life, friends, is boring. We must not say so.
After all, the sky flashes, the great sea yearns,
we ourselves flash and yearn,
and moreover my mother told me as a boy
(repeatingly) 'Ever to confess you're bored
means you have no

Inner Resources.' I conclude now I have no
inner resources, because I am heavy bored.
Peoples bore me,
literature bores me, especially great literature,
Henry bores me, with his plights & gripes
as bad as achilles,

who loves people and valiant art, which bores me.
And the tranquil hills, & gin, look like a drag
and somehow a dog
has taken itself & its tail considerably away
into mountains or sea or sky, leaving
behind: me, wag.

JOHN BERRYMAN

Dream Song 312

I have moved to Dublin to have it out with you,
majestic Shade, You whom I read so well
so many years ago,
did I read your lesson right? did I see through
your phases to the real? your heaven, your hell
did I enquire properly into?

For years then I forgot you, I put you down,
ingratitude is the necessary curse
of making things new:
I brought my family to see me through,
I brought my homage & my soft remorse,
I brought a book or two

only, including in the end your last
strange poems made under the shadow of death
Your high figures float
again across my mind and all your past
fills my walled garden with your honey breath
wherein I move, a mote.

WILLIAM SHAKESPEARE

from *Hamlet* (Act III, Scene i)

HAMLET:
   To be, or not to be – that is the question;
   Whether 'tis nobler in the mind to suffer
   The slings and arrows of outrageous fortune
   Or to take arms against a sea of troubles
   And by opposing end them. To die, to sleep –
   No more – and by a sleep to say we end
   The heartache and the thousand natural shocks
   That flesh is heir to. 'Tis a consummation
   Devoutly to be wished. To die, to sleep –
   To sleep – perchance to dream. Ay, there's the rub.
   For in that sleep of death what dreams may come
   When we have shuffled off this mortal coil
   Must give us pause. There's the respect
   That makes calamity of so long life.
   For who would bear the whips and scorns of time,
   Th'oppressor's wrong, the proud man's contumely,
   The pangs of despised love, the law's delay,
   The insolence of office, and the spurns
   That patient merit of th'unworthy takes,
   When he himself might his quietus make
   With a bare bodkin? Who would fardels bear,
   To grunt and sweat under a weary life,
   But that the dread of something after death,
   The undiscovered country, from whose bourn
   No traveller returns, puzzles the will,
   And makes us rather bear those ills we have
   Than fly to others that we know not of?
   Thus conscience does make cowards of us all;

And thus the native hue of resolution
Is sicklied o'er with the pale cast of thought,
And enterprises of great pitch and moment
With this regard their currents turn awry
And lose the name of action. Soft you now,
The fair Ophelia! – Nymph, in thy orisons
Be all my sins remembered.

Skunk Hour

(For Elizabeth Bishop)

Nautilus Island's hermit
heiress still lives through winter in her
    Spartan cottage;
her sheep still graze above the sea.
Her son's a bishop. Her farmer
is first selectman in our village;
she's in her dotage.

Thirsting for
the hierarchic privacy
of Queen Victoria's century,
she buys up all
the eyesores facing her shore,
and lets them fall.

The season's ill—
we've lost our summer millionaire,
who seemed to leap from an L. L. Bean
catalogue. His nine-knot yawl
was auctioned off to lobstermen.
A red fox stain covers Blue Hill.

And now our fairy
decorator brightens his shop for fall;
his fishnet's filled with orange cork,
orange, his cobbler's bench and awl;
there is no money in his work,
he'd rather marry.

One dark night,
my Tudor Ford climbed the hill's skull;
I watched for love-cars. Lights turned down,
they lay together, hull to hull,
where the graveyard shelves on the town. . . .
My mind's not right.

A car radio bleats,
"Love, O careless Love. . . ." I hear
my ill-spirit sob in each blood cell,
as if my hand were at its throat. . . .
I myself am hell;
nobody's here—

only skunks, that search
in the moonlight for a bite to eat.
They march on their soles up Main Street:
white stripes, moonstruck eyes' red fire
under the chalk-dry and spar spire
of the Trinitarian Church.

I stand on top
of our back steps and breathe the rich air—
a mother skunk with her column of kittens swills
    the garbage pail.
She jabs her wedge-head in a cup
of sour cream, drops her ostrich tail,
and will not scare.

from *Howl*

For Carl Solomon

I

I saw the best minds of my generation destroyed by madness,
    starving hysterical naked,
dragging themselves through the negro streets at dawn
    looking for an angry fix,
angelheaded hipsters burning for the ancient heavenly
    connection to the starry dynamo in the machinery of
    night,
who poverty and tatters and hollow-eyed and high sat up
    smoking in the supernatural darkness of cold-water flats
    floating across the tops of cities contemplating jazz,
who bared their brains to Heaven under the El and saw
    Mohammedan angels staggering on tenement roofs
    illuminated,
who passed through universities with radiant cool eyes
    hallucinating Arkansas and Blake-light tragedy among the
    scholars of war,
who were expelled from the academies for crazy &
    publishing obscene odes on the windows of the skull,
who cowered in unshaven rooms in underwear, burning their
    money in wastebaskets and listening to the Terror
    through the wall,
who got busted in their pubic beards returning through
    Laredo with a belt of marijuana for New York,
who ate fire in paint hotels or drank turpentine in Paradise
    Alley, death, or purgatoried their torsos night after night
with dreams, with drugs, with waking nightmares, alcohol
    and cock and endless balls,
incomparable blind streets of shuddering cloud and lightning

in the mind leaping toward poles of Canada & Paterson,
illuminating all the motionless world of Time between,
Peyote solidities of halls, backyard green tree cemetery
dawns, wine drunkenness over the rooftops, storefront
boroughs of teahead joyride neon blinking traffic light,
sun and moon and tree vibrations in the roaring winter
dusks of Brooklyn, ashcan rantings and kind king light of
mind,
who chained themselves to subways for the endless ride from
Battery to holy Bronx on benzedrine until the noise of
wheels and children brought them down shuddering
mouth-wracked and battered bleak of brain all drained of
brilliance in the drear light of Zoo,
who sank all night in submarine light of Bickford's floated
out and sat through the stale beer afternoon in desolate
Fugazzi's, listening to the crack of doom on the hydrogen
jukebox,
who talked continuously seventy hours from park to pad to
bar to Bellevue to museum to the Brooklyn Bridge,
a lost battalion of platonic conversationalists jumping down
the stoops off fire escapes off windowsills off Empire
State out of the moon,
yacketayakking screaming vomiting whispering facts and
memories and anecdotes and eyeball kicks and shocks of
hospitals and jails and wars,
whole intellects disgorged in total recall for seven days and
nights with brilliant eyes, meat for the Synagogue cast on
the pavement,
who vanished into nowhere Zen New Jersey leaving a trail of
ambiguous picture postcards of Atlantic City Hall,
suffering Eastern sweats and Tangerian bone-grindings and
migraines of China under junk-withdrawal in Newark's
bleak furnished room,
who wandered around and around at midnight in the railroad
yard wondering where to go, and went, leaving no
broken hearts

The Great Lover

I have been so great a lover: filled my days
So proudly with the splendour of Love's praise,
The pain, the calm, and the astonishment,
Desire illimitable, and still content,
And all dear names men use, to cheat despair,
For the perplexed and viewless streams that bear
Our hearts at random down the dark of life.
Now, ere the unthinking silence on that strife
Steals down, I would cheat drowsy Death so far,
My night shall be remembered for a star
That outshone all the suns of all men's days.
Shall I not crown them with immortal praise
Whom I have loved, who have given me, dared with me
High secrets, and in darkness knelt to see
The inenarrable godhead of delight?
Love is a flame: – we have beaconed the world's night,
A city: – and we have built it, these and I.
An emperor: – we have taught the world to die.
So, for their sakes I loved, ere I go hence,
And the high cause of Love's magnificence,
And to keep loyalties young, I'll write those names
Golden for ever, eagles, crying flames,
And set them as a banner, that men may know,
To dare the generations, burn, and blow
Out on the wind of Time, shining and streaming. . . .

These I have loved:
        White plates and cups, clean-gleaming,
Ringed with blue lines; and feathery, faery dust;
Wet roofs, beneath the lamp-light: the strong crust
Of friendly bread; and many-tasting food;
Rainbows; and the blue bitter smoke of wood;

And radiant raindrops couching in cool flowers;
And flowers themselves, that sway through sunny hours,
Dreaming of moths that drink them under the moon;
Then, the cool kindliness of sheets, that soon
Smooth away trouble; and the rough male kiss
Of blankets; grainy wood; live hair that is
Shining and free; blue-massing clouds; the keen
Unpassioned beauty of a great machine;
The benison of hot water; furs to touch;
The good smell of old clothes; and other such –
The comfortable smell of friendly fingers,
Hair's fragrance, and the musty reek that lingers
About dead leaves and last year's ferns. . . .
                                        Dear names,
And thousand other throng to me! Royal flames;
Sweet water's dimpling laugh from tap or spring;
Holes in the ground; and voices that do sing;
Voices in laughter, too; and body's pain,
Soon turned to peace; and the deep-panting train;
Firm sands; the little dulling edge of foam
That browns and dwindles as the wave goes home;
And washen stones, gay for an hour; the cold
Graveness of iron; moist black earthen mould;
Sleep; and high places; footprints in the dew;
And oaks; and brown horse-chestnuts, glossy-new;
And new-peeled sticks; and shining pools on grass;-
All these have been my loves. And these shall pass.
Whatever passes not, in the great hour,
Nor all my passion, all my prayers, have power
To hold them with me through the gate of Death.
They'll play deserter, turn with the traitor breath,
Break the high bond we made, and sell Love's trust
And sacramented covenant to the dust.
——Oh, never a doubt but, somewhere, I shall wake,
And give what's left of love again, and make
New friends, now strangers. . . .
                                        But the best I've known
Stays here, and changes, breaks, grows old, is blown

About the winds of the world, and fades from brains
Of living men, and dies.

                                      Nothing remains.
O dear my loves, O faithless, once again
This one last gift I give: that after men
Shall know, and later lovers, far-removed,
Praise you, 'All these were lovely'; say, 'He loved.'

The Old Vicarage, Grantchester

(*Café des Westens, Berlin, May 1912*)

Just now the lilac is in bloom,
All before my little room;
And in my flower-beds, I think,
Smile the carnation and the pink;
And down the borders, well I know,
The poppy and the pansy blow –
Oh! there the chestnuts, summer through,
Beside the river make for you
A tunnel of green gloom, and sleep
Deeply above; and green and deep
The stream mysterious glides beneath,
Green as a dream and deep as death.
– Oh, damn! I know it! and I know
How the May fields all golden show,
And when the day is young and sweet,
Gild gloriously the bare feet.
That run to bathe –
                    Du lieber Gott!

Here am I, sweating, sick, and hot,
And there the shadowed waters fresh
Lean up to embrace the naked flesh.
Temperamentvoll German Jews
Drink beer around – and *there* the dews
Are soft beneath a morn of gold.
Here tulips bloom as they are told;
Unkempt about those hedges blows
An English unofficial rose;

And there the unregulated sun
Slopes down to rest when day is done,
And wakes a vague unpunctual star,
A slippered Hesper; and there are
Meads towards Haslingfield and Coton
Where *das Betreten's* not *verboten*.

Ειυε γεψοιμηψ . . . would I were
In Grantchester, in Grantchester!
Some, it may be, can get in touch
With Nature there, or Earth, or such.
And clever modern men have seen
A Faun a-peeping through the green,
And felt the Classics were not dead,
To glimpse a Naiad's reedy head,
Or hear the Goat-foot piping low: –
But these are things I do not know.
I only know that you may lie
Day-long and watch the Cambridge sky,
And, flower-lulled in sleepy grass,
Hear the cool lapse of hours pass,
Until the centuries blend and blur
In Grantchester, in Grantchester –
Still in the dawnlit waters cool
His ghostly Lordship swims his pool,
And tries the strokes, essays the tricks,
Long learnt on Hellespont, or Styx.
Dan Chaucer hears his river still
Chatter beneath a phantom mill.

Tennyson notes, with studious eye,
How Cambridge waters hurry by –
And in that garden, black and white,
Creep whispers through the grass all night;
And spectral dance, before the dawn,
A hundred Vicars down the lawn;

Curates, long dust, will come and go
On lissom, clerical, printless toe;
And oft between the boughs is seen
The sly shade of a Rural Dean –
Till, at a shiver in the skies,
Vanishing with Satanic cries,
The prim ecclesiastic rout
Leaves but a startled sleeper-out,
Grey heavens, the first bird's drowsy calls,
The falling house that never falls.

God! I will pack, and take a train,
And get me to England once again!
For England's the one land, I know,
Where men with Splendid Hearts may go;
And Cambridgeshire, of all England,
The shire for Men who Understand;
And of *that* district I prefer
The lovely hamlet Grantchester.
For Cambridge people rarely smile,
Being urban, squat, and packed with guile;
And Royston men in the far South
Are black and fierce and strange of mouth;
At Over they fling oaths at one,
And worse than oaths at Trumpington,
And Ditton girls are mean and dirty,
And there's none in Harston under thirty,
And folks in Shelford and those parts
Have twisted lips and twisted hearts,
And Barton men make Cockney rhymes,
And Coton's full of nameless crimes,
And things are done you'd not believe
At Madingley, on Christmas Eve.
Strong men have run for miles and miles,
When one from Cherry Hinton smiles;

Strong men have blanched, and shot their wives,
Rather than send them to St Ives;
Strong men have cried like babes, bydam,
To hear what happened at Babraham.
But Grantchester! ah, Grantchester!
There's peace and holy quiet there,
Great clouds along pacific skies,
And men and women with straight eyes,
Lithe children lovelier than a dream,
A bosky wood, a slumbrous stream,
And little kindly winds that creep
Round twilight corners, half asleep.
In Grantchester their skins are white;
They bathe by day, they bathe by night;
The women there do all they ought;
The men observe the Rules of Thought.
They love the Good; they worship Truth;
They laugh uproariously in youth;
(And when they get to feeling old,
They up and shoot themselves, I'm told) –

      Ah God! to see the branches stir
Across the moon at Grantchester!
To smell the thrilling-sweet and rotten
Unforgettable, unforgotten
River-smell, and hear the breeze
Sobbing in the little trees.
Say, do the elm-clumps greatly stand
Still guardians of that holy land?
The chestnuts shade, in reverend dream,
The yet unacademic stream?
Is dawn a secret shy and cold
Anadyomene, silver-gold?
And sunset still a golden sea
From Haslingfield to Madingley?

And after, ere the night is born,
Do hares come out about the corn?
Oh, is the water sweet and cool,
Gentle and brown, above the pool?
And laughs the immortal river still
Under the mill, under the mill?
Say, is there Beauty yet to find?
And Certainty? and Quiet kind?
Deep meadows yet, for to forget
The lies, and truths, and pain? – oh! yet
Stands the Church clock at ten to three?
And is there honey still for tea?

PHILIP LARKIN

The Whitsun Weddings

That Whitsun, I was late getting away:
    Not till about
One-twenty on the sunlit Saturday
Did my three-quarters-empty train pull out,
All windows down, all cushions hot, all sense
Of being in a hurry gone. We ran
Behind the backs of houses, crossed a street
Of blinding windscreens, smelt the fish-dock; thence
The river's level drifting breadth began,
Where sky and Lincolnshire and water meet.

All afternoon, through the tall heat that slept
    For miles inland,
A slow and stopping curve southwards we kept.
Wide farms went by, short-shadowed cattle, and
Canals with floatings of industrial froth;
A hothouse flashed uniquely: hedges dipped
And rose: and now and then a smell of grass
Displaced the reek of buttoned carriage-cloth
Until the next town, new and nondescript,
Approached with acres of dismantled cars.

At first, I didn't notice what a noise
    The weddings made
Each station that we stopped at: sun destroys
The interest of what's happening in the shade,
And down the long cool platforms whoops and skirls
I took for porters larking with the mails,
And went on reading. Once we started, though,
We passed them, grinning and pomaded, girls
In parodies of fashion, heels and veils,
All posed irresolutely, watching us go,

As if out on the end of an event
   Waving goodbye
To something that survived it. Struck, I leant
More promptly out next time, more curiously,
And saw it all again in different terms:
The fathers with broad belts under their suits
And seamy foreheads; mothers loud and fat;
An uncle shouting smut; and then the perms,
The nylon gloves and jewellery-substitutes,
The lemons, mauves, and olive-ochres that

Marked off the girls unreally from the rest.
   Yes, from cafés
And banquet-halls up yards, and bunting-dressed
Coach-party annexes, the wedding-days
Were coming to an end. All down the line
Fresh couples climbed aboard: the rest stood round;
The last confetti and advice were thrown,
And, as we moved, each face seemed to define
Just what it saw departing: children frowned
At something dull; fathers had never known

Success so huge and wholly farcical;
   The women shared
The secret like a happy funeral;
While girls, gripping their handbags tighter, stared
At a religious wounding. Free at last,
And loaded with the sum of all they saw,
We hurried towards London, shuffling gouts of steam.
Now fields were building-plots, and poplars cast
Long shadows over major roads, and for
Some fifty minutes, that in time would seem

Just long enough to settle hats and say
   I nearly died,
A dozen marriages got under way.
They watched the landscape, sitting side by side
– An Odeon went past, a cooling tower,

And someone running up to bowl – and none
Thought of the others they would never meet
Or how their lives would all contain this hour.
I thought of London spread out in the sun,
Its postal districts packed like squares of wheat:

There we were aimed. And as we raced across
  Bright knots of rail
Past standing Pullmans, walls of blackened moss
Came close, and it was nearly done, this frail
Travelling coincidence; and what it held
Stood ready to be loosed with all the power
That being changed can give. We slowed again,
And as the tightened brakes took hold, there swelled
A sense of falling, like an arrow-shower
Sent out of sight, somewhere becoming rain.

PHILIP LARKIN

This Be the Verse

They fuck you up, your mum and dad.
  They may not mean to, but they do.
They fill you with the faults they had
  And add some extra, just for you.

But they were fucked up in their turn
  By fools in old-style hats and coats,
Who half the time were soppy-stern
  And half at one another's throats.

Man hands on misery to man.
  It deepens like a coastal shelf.
Get out as early as you can,
  And don't have any kids yourself.

An Arundel Tomb

Side by side, their faces blurred,
The earl and countess lie in stone,
Their proper habits vaguely shown
As jointed armour, stiffened pleat,
And that faint hint of the absurd –
The little dogs under their feet.

Such plainness of the pre-baroque
Hardly involves the eye, until
It meets his left-hand gauntlet, still
Clasped empty in the other; and
One sees, with a sharp tender shock,
His hand withdrawn, holding her hand.

They would not think to lie so long.
Such faithfulness in effigy
Was just a detail friends would see:
A sculptor's sweet commissioned grace
Thrown off in helping to prolong
The Latin names around the base.

They would not guess how early in
Their supine stationary voyage
The air would change to soundless damage,
Turn the old tenantry away;
How soon succeeding eyes begin
To look, not read. Rigidly they

Persisted, linked, through lengths and breadths
Of time. Snow fell, undated. Light
Each summer thronged the glass. A bright
Litter of birdcalls strewed the same
Bone-riddled ground. And up the paths
The endless altered people came,

Washing at their identity.
Now, helpless in the hollow of
An unarmorial age, a trough
Of smoke in slow suspended skeins
Above their scrap of history,
Only an attitude remains:

Time has transfigured them into
Untruth. The stone fidelity
They hardly meant has come to be
Their final blazon, and to prove
Our almost-instinct almost true:
What will survive of us is love.

PHILIP LARKIN

Friday Night in the Royal Station Hotel

Light spreads darkly downwards from the high
Clusters of lights over empty chairs
That face each other, coloured differently.
Through open doors, the dining-room declares
A larger loneliness of knives and glass
And silence laid like carpet. A porter reads
An unsold evening paper. Hours pass,
And all the salesmen have gone back to Leeds,
Leaving full ashtrays in the Conference Room.

In shoeless corridors, the lights burn. How
Isolated, like a fort, it is –
The headed paper, made for writing home
(If home existed) letters of exile: *Now
Night comes on. Waves fold behind villages.*

DON PATERSON

'96

her sleek
thigh
on my
cheek

a flayed
tongue
in the wrong
head

no poem
all year
but its dumb

inverse
sow's ear
silk purse

DON PATERSON

The Thread

Jamie made his landing in the world
so hard he ploughed straight back into the earth.
They caught him by the thread of his one breath
and pulled him up. They don't know how it held.
And so today I thank what higher will
brought us to here, to you and me and Russ,
the great twin-engined swaying wingspan of us
roaring down the back of Kirrie Hill

and your two-year-old lungs somehow out-revving
every engine in the universe.
All that trouble just to turn up dead
was all I thought that long week. Now the thread
is holding all of us: look at our tiny house,
son, the white dot of your mother waving.

SEAMUS HEANEY

The Skunk

Up, black, striped and demasked like the chasuble
At a funeral mass, the skunk's tail
Paraded the skunk. Night after night
I expected her like a visitor.

The refrigerator whinnied into silence.
My desk light softened beyond the verandah.
Small oranges loomed in the orange tree.
I began to be tense as a voyeur.

After eleven years I was composing
Love-letters again, broaching the 'wife'
Like a stored cask, as if its slender vowel
Had mutated into the night earth and air

Of California. The beautiful, useless
Tang of eucalyptus spelt your absence.
The aftermath of a mouthful of wine
Was like inhaling you off a cold pillow.

And there she was, the intent and glamorous,
Ordinary, mysterious skunk,
Mythologized, demythologized,
Snuffing the boards five feet beyond me.

It all came back to me last night, stirred
By the sootfall of your things at bedtime,
Your head-down, tail-up hunt in a bottom drawer
For the black plunge-line nightdress.

SEAMUS HEANEY

Casting and Gathering

for Ted Hughes

Years and years ago, these sounds took sides:

On the left bank, a green silk tapered cast
Went whispering through the air, saying *hush*
And *lush*, entirely free, no matter whether
It swished above the hayfield or the river.

On the right bank, like a speeded-up corncrake,
A sharp ratcheting went on and on
Cutting across the stillness as another
Fisherman gathered line-lengths off his reel.

I am still standing there, awake and dreamy,
I have grown older and can see them both
Moving their arms and rods, working away,
Each one absorbed, proofed by the sounds he's making.

One sound is saying. "You are not worth tuppence,
But neither is anybody. Watch it! Be severe."
The other says, "Go with it! Give and swerve.
You are everything you feel beside the river."

I love hushed air. I trust contrariness.
Years and years go past and I do not move
For I see that when one man casts, the other gathers
And then *vice versa*, without changing sides.

Morning Song

Love set you going like a fat gold watch.
The midwife slapped your footsoles, and your bald cry
Took its place among the elements.

Our voices echo, magnifying your arrival. New statue.
In a drafty museum, your nakedness
Shadows our safety. We stand round blankly as walls.

I'm no more your mother
Than the cloud that distills a mirror to reflect its own slow
Effacement at the wind's hand.

All night your moth-breath
Flickers among the flat pink roses. I wake to listen:
A far sea moves in my ear.

One cry, and I stumble from bed, cow-heavy and floral
In my Victorian nightgown.
Your mouth opens clean as a cat's. The window square

Whitens and swallows its dull stars. And now you try
Your handful of notes;
The clear vowels rise like balloons.

Lady Lazarus

I have done it again.
One year in every ten
I manage it—

A sort of walking miracle, my skin
Bright as a Nazi lampshade,
My right foot

A paperweight,
My face a featureless, fine
Jew linen.

Peel off the napkin
O my enemy.
Do I terrify?—

The nose, the eye pits, the full set of teeth?
The sour breath
Will vanish in a day.

Soon, soon the flesh
The grave cave ate will be
At home on me

And I a smiling woman.
I am only thirty.
And like the cat I have nine times to die.

This is Number Three.
What a trash
To annihilate each decade.

What a million filaments.
The peanut-crunching crowd
Shoves in to see

Them unwrap me hand and foot—
The big strip tease.
Gentlemen, ladies

These are my hands
My knees.
I may be skin and bone,

Nevertheless, I am the same, identical woman.
The first time it happened I was ten.
It was an accident.

The second time I meant
To last it out and not come back at all.
I rocked shut

As a seashell.
They had to call and call
And pick the worms off me like sticky pearls.

Dying
Is an art, like everything else.
I do it exceptionally well.

I do it so it feels like hell.
I do it so it feels real.
I guess you could say I've a call.

It's easy enough to do it in a cell.
It's easy enough to do it and stay put.
It's the theatrical

Comeback in broad day
To the same place, the same face, the same brute
Amused shout:

'A miracle!'
That knocks me out.
There is a charge

For the eyeing of my scars, there is a charge
For the hearing of my heart—
It really goes.

And there is a charge, a very large charge
For a word or a touch
Or a bit of blood

Or a piece of my hair or my clothes.
So, so, Herr Doktor.
So, Herr Enemy.

I am your opus,
I am your valuable,
The pure gold baby

That melts to a shriek.
I turn and burn.
Do not think I underestimate your great concern.

Ash, ash—
You poke and stir.
Flesh, bone, there is nothing there—

A cake of soap,
A wedding ring,
A gold filling.

Herr God, Herr Lucifer
Beware
Beware.

Out of the ash
I rise with my red hair
And I eat men like air.

Ariel

Stasis in darkness.
Then the substanceless blue
Pour of tor and distances.

God's lioness,
How one we grow,
Pivot of heels and knees!—The furrow

Splits and passes, sister to
The brown arc
Of the neck I cannot catch,

Nigger-eye
Berries cast dark
Hooks—

Black sweet blood mouthfuls,
Shadows.
Something else

Hauls me through air—
Thighs, hair;
Flakes from my heels.

White
Godiva, I unpeel –
Dead hands, dead stringencies.

And now I
Foam to wheat, a glitter of seas.
The child's cry

Melts in the wall.
And I
Am the arrow,

The dew that flies
Suicidal, at one with the drive
Into the red

Eye, the cauldron of morning.

CERYS MATTHEWS

Britain in Poetry

'I will do better towards thee,
To celebrate thee in poetic eulogy.'

Aneirin, from *Y Gododdin*

ANEIRIN

from Y *Gododdin*

I

Of manly disposition was the youth,
Valour had he in the tumult;
Fleet thick-maned chargers
Were under the thigh of the illustrious youth;
A shield, light and broad,
Was on the slender swift flank,
A sword, blue and bright,
Golden spurs, and ermine.
It is not by me
That hatred shall be shown to thee;
I will do better towards thee,
To celebrate thee in poetic eulogy.
Sooner hadst thou gone to the bloody bier
Than to the nuptial feast;
Sooner hadst thou gone to be food for ravens
Than to the conflict of spears;
Thou beloved friend of Owain!
Wrong it is that he should be under ravens.
It is evident in what region
The only son of Marro was killed.

II

Caeawg, the leader, wherever he came,
Breathless in the presence of a maid would he
    distribute the mead;
The front of his shield was pierced, when he heard
The shout of battle, he would give no quarter
    wherever he pursued;
He would not retreat from the combat, until he
    caused

Blood to stream; like rushes would he hew down the men
  who would not yield.
The Gododdin does not relate, in the land of Mordai,
Before the tents of Madawg, when he returned,
Of but one man in a hundred that came back.

III

Caeawg, the combatant, the stay of his country,
Whose attack is like the rush of the eagle into the sea,
  when allured by his prey;
He formed a compact, his signal was observed;
Better was his resolution performed: he retreated not
Before the host of Gododdin, at the close of day.
With confidence he pressed upon the conflict of
  Manawyd;
And regarded neither spear nor shield.
There is not to be found a habitation that abounded in
  dainties,
That has been kept from the attack of the warriors.

IV

Caeawg, the leader, the wolf of the strand,
Amber wreaths encircled his brow;
Precious was the amber, worth wine from the horn.
He repelled the violence of ignoble men, and blood
  trickled down;
For Gwynedd and the North would have come to his
  share,
By the advice of the son of Ysgyrran,
Who wore the broken shield.

V

Caeawg, the leader, armed was he in the noisy conflict;
His was the foremost part of the advanced division, in
  front of the hosts.
Before his blades fell five battalions.
Of the men of Deivyr and Brenneich, uttering groans:
Twenty hundred perished in one hour.

Sooner did his flesh go to the wolf, than he to the nuptial
   feast;
He sooner became food for the raven, than approached
   the altar;
Before he entered the conflict of spears, his blood
   streamed to the ground.
It was the price of mead in the hall, amidst the throng.
Hyveidd Hir shall be celebrated as long as there will be a
   minstrel.

VI

The men went to Gododdin with laughter and
   sprightliness,
Bitter were they in the battle, displaying their blades;
A short year they remained in peace.
The son of Bodgad, by the energy of his hand, caused a
   throbbing.
Though they went to churches to do penance,
The old, and the young, and the bold-handed,
The inevitable strife of death was to pierce them.

VII

The men went to Gododdin, laughing as they moved:
A gloomy disaster befell their army;
Thou slayest them with blades, without much noise:
Thou, powerful pillar of living right, causest stillness.

VIII

The men went to Catraeth, loquacious was their host;
Fresh mead was their feast, and also their poison.
Three hundred were contending with weapons;
And after sportive mirth, stillness ensued!
Though they went to churches to do penance,
The inevitable strife of death was to pierce them.

IX

The men went to Catraeth, fed with mead, and drunk.
Firm and vigorous; it were wrong if I neglected to praise
 them.
Around the red, mighty, and murky blades
Obstinately and fiercely fought the dogs of war.
If I had judged you to be on the side of the tribe of
 Brenneich,
Not the phantom of a man would I have left alive.
A friend I have lost, myself being unhurt;
He openly opposed the terrible chief –
The magnanimous hero did not seek the dowry of his
 father-in-law;
The son of Cian of Maen Gwyngwn.

X

The men went to Catraeth with the dawn;
They dealt peaceably with those who feared them.
A hundred thousand and three hundred engaged in
 mutual overthrow.
Drenched in gore they served as butts for lances;
Their post they most manfully defended
Before the retinue of Mynyddawg Mwynvawr.

DYLAN THOMAS

The force that through the green fuse

The force that through the green fuse drives the flower
Drives my green age; that blasts the roots of trees
Is my destroyer.
And I am dumb to tell the crooked rose
My youth is bent by the same wintry fever.

The force that drives the water through the rocks
Drives my red blood; that dries the mouthing streams
Turns mine to wax.
And I am dumb to mouth unto my veins
How at the mountain spring the same mouth sucks.

The hand that whirls the water in the pool
Stirs the quicksand; that ropes the blowing wind
Hauls my shroud sail.
And I am dumb to tell the hanging man
How of my clay is made the hangman's lime.

The lips of time leech to the fountain head;
Love drips and gathers, but the fallen blood
Shall calm her sores.
And I am dumb to tell a weather's wind
How time has ticked a heaven round the stars.

And I am dumb to tell the lover's tomb
How at my sheet goes the same crooked worm.

DYLAN THOMAS

After the funeral

(In memory of Ann Jones)

After the funeral, mule praises, brays,
Windshake of sailshaped ears, muffle-toed tap
Tap happily of one peg in the thick
Grave's foot, blinds down the lids, the teeth in black,
The spittled eyes, the salt ponds in the sleeves,
Morning smack of the spade that wakes up sleep,
Shakes a desolate boy who slits his throat
In the dark of the coffin and sheds dry leaves,
That breaks one bone to light with a judgment clout,
After the feast of tear-stuffed time and thistles
In a room with a stuffed fox and a stale fern,
I stand, for this memorial's sake, alone
In the snivelling hours with dead, humped Ann
Whose hooded, fountain heart once fell in puddles
Round the parched worlds of Wales and drowned
    each sun
(Though this for her is a monstrous image blindly
Magnified out of praise; her death was a still drop;
She would not have me sinking in the holy
Flood of her heart's fame; she would lie dumb and
    deep
And need no druid of her broken body).
But I, Ann's bard on a raised hearth, call all
The seas to service that her wood-tongued virtue
Babble like a bellbuoy over the hymning heads,
Bow down the walls of the ferned and foxy woods
That her love sing and swing through a brown chapel,
Bless her bent spirit with four, crossing birds.
Her flesh was meek as milk, but this skyward statue
With the wild breast and blessed and giant skull

Is carved from her in a room with a wet window
In a fiercely mourning house in a crooked year.
I know her scrubbed and sour humble hands
Lie with religion in their cramp, her threadbare
Whisper in a damp word, her wits drilled hollow,
Her fist of a face died clenched on a round pain;
And sculptured Ann is seventy years of stone.
These cloud-sopped, marble hands, this monumental
Argument of the hewn voice, gesture and psalm
Storm me forever over her grave until
The stuffed lung of the fox twitch and cry Love
And the strutting fern lay seeds on the black sill.

DYLAN THOMAS

The hunchback in the park

The hunchback in the park
A solitary mister
Propped between trees and water
From the opening of the garden lock
That lets the trees and water enter
Until the Sunday sombre bell at dark

Eating bread from a newspaper
Drinking water from the chained cup
That the children filled with gravel
In the fountain basin where I sailed my ship
Slept at night in a dog kennel
But nobody chained him up.

Like the park birds he came early
Like the water he sat down
And Mister they called Hey mister
The truant boys from the town
Running when he had heard them clearly
On out of sound

Past lake and rockery
Laughing when he shook his paper
Hunchbacked in mockery
Through the loud zoo of the willow groves
Dodging the park keeper
With his stick that picked up leaves.

And the old dog sleeper
Alone between nurses and swans
While the boys among willows
Made the tigers jump out of their eyes
To roar on the rockery stones
And the groves were blue with sailors

Made all day until bell time
A woman figure without fault
Straight as a young elm
Straight and tall from his crooked bones
That she might stand in the night
After the locks and chains

All night in the unmade park
After the railings and shrubberies
The birds the grass the trees the lake
And the wild boys innocent as strawberries
Had followed the hunchback
To his kennel in the dark.

DYLAN THOMAS

In my craft or sullen art

In my craft or sullen art
Exercised in the still night
When only the moon rages
And the lovers lie abed
With all their griefs in their arms,
I labour by singing light
Not for ambition or bread
Or the strut and trade of charms
On the ivory stages
But for the common wages
Of their most secret heart.

Not for the proud man apart
From the raging moon I write
On these spindrift pages
Nor for the towering dead
With their nightingales and psalms
But for the lovers, their arms
Round the griefs of the ages,
Who pay no praise or wages
Nor heed my craft or art.

DYLAN THOMAS

Fern Hill

Now as I was young and easy under the apple boughs
About the lilting house and happy as the grass was green,
    The night above the dingle starry,
        Time let me hail and climb
    Golden in the heydays of his eyes,
And honoured among wagons I was prince of the apple towns
And once below a time I lordly had the trees and leaves
        Trail with daisies and barley
    Down the rivers of the windfall light.

And as I was green and carefree, famous among the barns
About the happy yard and singing as the farm was home,
    In the sun that is young once only,
        Time let me play and be
    Golden in the mercy of his means,
And green and golden I was huntsman and herdsman, the calves
Sang to my horn, the foxes on the hills barked clear and cold,
        And the sabbath rang slowly
    In the pebbles of the holy streams.

All the sun long it was running, it was lovely, the hay
Fields high as the house, the tunes from the chimneys, it was air
    And playing, lovely and watery
        And fire green as grass.
    And nightly under the simple stars
As I rode to sleep the owls were bearing the farm away,
All the moon long I heard, blessed among stables, the nightjars
        Flying with the ricks, and the horses
        Flashing into the dark.

And then to awake, and the farm, like a wanderer white
With the dew, come back, the cock on his shoulder: it was all
    Shining, it was Adam and maiden,
        The sky gathered again
    And the sun grew round that very day.
So it must have been after the birth of the simple light
In the first, spinning place, the spellbound horses walking warm
     Out of the whinnying green stable
        On to the fields of praise.

And honoured among foxes and pheasants by the gay house
Under the new made clouds and happy as the heart was long,
    In the sun born over and over,
        I ran my heedless ways,
    My wishes raced through the house high hay
And nothing I cared, at my sky blue trades, that time allows
In all his tuneful turning so few and such morning songs
   · Before the children green and golden
        Follow him out of grace,

Nothing I cared, in the lamb white days, that time would take me
Up to the swallow thronged loft by the shadow of my hand,
    In the moon that is always rising,
        Nor that riding to sleep
    I should hear him fly with the high fields
And wake to the farm forever fled from the childless land.
Oh as I was young and easy in the mercy of his means,
        Time held me green and dying
    Though I sang in my chains like the sea.

DYLAN THOMAS

Do not go gentle into that good night

Do not go gentle into that good night,
Old age should burn and rave at close of day;
Rage, rage against the dying of the light.

Though wise men at their end know dark is right,
Because their words had forked no lightning they
Do not go gentle into that good night.

Good men, the last wave by, crying how bright
Their frail deeds might have danced in a green bay,
Rage, rage against the dying of the light.

Wild men who caught and sang the sun in flight,
And learn, too late, they grieved it on its way,
Do not go gentle into that good night.

Grave men, near death, who see with blinding sight
Blind eyes could blaze like meteors and be gay,
Rage, rage against the dying of the light.

And you, my father, there on the sad height,
Curse, bless, me now with your fierce tears, I pray.
Do not go gentle into that good night.
Rage, rage against the dying of the light.

DYLAN THOMAS

And death shall have no dominion

And death shall have no dominion.
Dead men naked they shall be one
With the man in the wind and the west moon;
When their bones are picked clean and the clean
    bones gone,
They shall have stars at elbow and foot;
Though they go mad they shall be sane,
Though they sink through the sea they shall rise
    again;
Though lovers be lost love shall not;
And death shall have no dominion.

And death shall have no dominion.
Under the windings of the sea
They lying long shall not die windily;
Twisting on racks when sinews give way,
Strapped to a wheel, yet they shall not break;
Faith in their hands shall snap in two,
And the unicorn evils run them through;
Split all ends up they shan't crack;
And death shall have no dominion.

And death shall have no dominion.
No more may gulls cry at their ears
Or waves break loud on the seashores;
Where blew a flower may a flower no more
Lift its head to the blows of the rain;
Though they be mad and dead as nails,
Heads of the characters hammer through daisies;
Break in the sun till the sun breaks down,
And death shall have no dominion.

IDRIS DAVIES

The Bells of Rhymney

O, what will you give me?
Say the sad bells of Rhymney.

Is there hope for the future?
Cry the brown bells of Merthyr.

Who made the mineowner?
Say the black bells of Rhondda.

And who robbed the miner?
Cry the grim bells of Blaina.

They will plunder willy-nilly,
Cry the bells of Caerphilly.

They have fangs, they have teeth!
Shout the loud bells of Neath.

To the south, things are sullen,
Say the pink bells of Brecon.

Even God is uneasy,
Say the moist bells of Swansea.

Put the vandals in court!
Cry the bells of Newport.

And would be well if—if—if—
Say the green bells of Cardiff.

Why so worried, sisters, why?
Sing the silver bells of Wye.

W. B. YEATS

Down by the Salley Gardens

Down by the salley gardens my love and I did meet;
She passed the salley gardens with little snow-white feet.
She bid me take love easy, as the leaves grow on the tree;
But I, being young and foolish, with her would not agree.

In a field by the river my love and I did stand,
And on my leaning shoulder she laid her snow-white hand.
She bid me take life easy, as the grass grows on the weirs;
But I was young and foolish, and now am full of tears.

W. B. YEATS

The Song of Wandering Aengus

I went out to the hazel wood,
Because a fire was in my head,
And cut and peeled a hazel wand,
And hooked a berry to a thread;
And when white moths were on the wing,
And moth-like stars were flickering out,
I dropped the berry in a stream
And caught a little silver trout.

When I had laid it on the floor
I went to blow the fire aflame,
But something rustled on the floor,
And some one called me by my name:
It had become a glimmering girl
With apple blossom in her hair
Who called me by my name and ran
And faded through the brightening air.

Though I am old with wandering
Through hollow lands and hilly lands,
I will find out where she has gone,
And kiss her lips and take her hands;
And walk among long dappled grass,
And pluck till time and times are done
The silver apples of the moon,
The golden apples of the sun.

The Wild Swans at Coole

The trees are in their autumn beauty,
The woodland paths are dry,
Under the October twilight the water
Mirrors a still sky;
Upon the brimming water among the stones
Are nine-and-fifty swans.

The nineteenth autumn has come upon me
Since I first made my count;
I saw, before I had well finished,
All suddenly mount
And scatter wheeling in great broken rings
Upon their clamorous wings.

I have looked upon those brilliant creatures,
And now my heart is sore.
All's changed since I, hearing at twilight,
The first time on this shore,
The bell-beat of their wings above my head,
Trod with a lighter tread.

Unwearied still, lover by lover,
They paddle in the cold
Companionable streams or climb the air;
Their hearts have not grown old;
Passion or conquest, wander where they will,
Attend upon them still.

But now they drift on the still water,
Mysterious, beautiful;
Among what rushes will they build,
By what lake's edge or pool
Delight men's eyes when I awake some day
To find they have flown away?

Easter, 1916

I have met them at close of day
Coming with vivid faces
From counter or desk among grey
Eighteenth-century houses.
I have passed with a nod of the head
Or polite meaningless words,
Or have lingered awhile and said
Polite meaningless words,
And thought before I had done
Of a mocking tale or a gibe
To please a companion
Around the fire at the club,
Being certain that they and I
But lived where motley is worn:
All changed, changed utterly:
A terrible beauty is born.

That woman's days were spent
In ignorant good-will,
Her nights in argument
Until her voice grew shrill.
What voice more sweet than hers
When, young and beautiful,
She rode to harriers?
This man had kept a school
And rode our wingèd horse;
This other his helper and friend
Was coming into his force;
He might have won fame in the end,
So sensitive his nature seemed,
So daring and sweet his thought.
This other man I had dreamed

A drunken, vainglorious lout.
He had done most bitter wrong
To some who are near my heart,
Yet I number him in the song;
He, too, has resigned his part
In the casual comedy;
He, too, has been changed in his turn,
Transformed utterly:
A terrible beauty is born.

Hearts with one purpose alone
Through summer and winter seem
Enchanted to a stone
To trouble the living stream.
The horse that comes from the road,
The rider, the birds that range
From cloud to tumbling cloud,
Minute by minute they change;
A shadow of cloud on the stream
Changes minute by minute;
A horse-hoof slides on the brim,
And a horse plashes within it;
The long-legged moor-hens dive,
And hens to moor-cocks call;
Minute by minute they live:
The stone's in the midst of all.

Too long a sacrifice
Can make a stone of the heart.
O when may it suffice?
That is Heaven's part, our part
To murmur name upon name,
As a mother names her child
When sleep at last has come
On limbs that had run wild.
What is it but nightfall?
No, no, not night but death;
Was it needless death after all?

For England may keep faith
For all that is done and said.
We know their dream; enough
To know they dreamed and are dead;
And what if excess of love
Bewildered them till they died?
I write it out in a verse –
MacDonagh and MacBride
And Connolly and Pearse
Now and in time to be,
Wherever green is worn,
Are changed, changed utterly:
A terrible beauty is born.

W. B. YEATS

Under Ben Bulben

I

Swear by what the Sages spoke
Round the Mareotic Lake
That the Witch of Atlas knew,
Spoke and set the cocks a-crow.

Swear by those horsemen, by those women,
Complexion and form prove superhuman,
That pale, long visaged company
That airs an immortality
Completeness of their passions won;
Now they ride the wintry dawn
Where Ben Bulben sets the scene.

Here's the gist of what they mean.

II

Many times man lives and dies
Between his two eternities,
That of race and that of soul,
And ancient Ireland knew it all.
Whether man dies in his bed
Or the rifle knocks him dead,
A brief parting from those dear
Is the worst man has to fear.
Though grave-diggers' toil is long,
Sharp their spades, their muscle strong,
They but thrust their buried men
Back in the human mind again.

You that Mitchel's prayer have heard
'Send war in our time, O Lord!'
Know that when all words are said
And a man is fighting mad,
Something drops from eyes long blind
He completes his partial mind,
For an instant stands at ease,
Laughs aloud, his heart at peace,
Even the wisest man grows tense
With some sort of violence
Before he can accomplish fate
Know his work or choose his mate.

IV

Poet and sculptor do the work
Nor let the modish painter shirk
What his great forefathers did,
Bring the soul of man to God,
Make him fill the cradles right.

Measurement began our might:
Forms a stark Egyptian thought,
Forms that gentler Phidias wrought.

Michael Angelo left a proof
On the Sistine Chapel roof,
Where but half-awakened Adam
Can disturb globe-trotting Madam
Till her bowels are in heat,
Proof that there's a purpose set
Before the secret working mind:
Profane perfection of mankind.

Quattrocento put in paint,
On backgrounds for a God or Saint,
Gardens where a soul's at ease;

Where everything that meets the eye
Flowers and grass and cloudless sky
Resemble forms that are, or seem
When sleepers wake and yet still dream,
And when it's vanished still declare,
With only bed and bedstead there,
That Heavens had opened.

                    Gyres run on;
When that greater dream had gone
Calvert and Wilson, Blake and Claude
Prepared a rest for the people of God,
Palmer's phrase, but after that
Confusion fell upon our thought.

V

Irish poets learn your trade
Sing whatever is well made,
Scorn the sort now growing up
All out of shape from toe to top,
Their unremembering hearts and heads
Base-born products of base beds.
Sing the peasantry, and then
Hard-riding country gentlemen,
The holiness of monks, and after
Porter-drinkers' randy laughter;
Sing the lords and ladies gay
That were beaten into the clay
Through seven heroic centuries;
Cast your mind on other days
That we in coming days may be
Still the indomitable Irishry.

VI

Under bare Ben Bulben's head
In Drumcliff churchyard Yeats is laid,
An ancestor was rector there
Long years ago; a church stands near,

By the road an ancient Cross.
No marble, no conventional phrase,
On limestone quarried near the spot
By his command these words are cut:

> Cast a cold eye
> On life, on death.
> Horseman, pass by!

W. B. YEATS

The Song of the Happy Shepherd

The woods of Arcady are dead,
And over is their antique joy;
Of old the world on dreaming fed;
Grey Truth is now her painted toy;
Yet still she turns her restless head:
But O, sick children of the world,
Of all the many changing things
In dreary dancing past us whirled,
To the cracked tune that Chronos sings,
Words alone are certain good.
Where are now the warring kings,
Word be-mockers? – By the Rood
Where are now the warring kings?
An idle word is now their glory,
By the stammering schoolboy said,
Reading some entangled story:
The kings of the old time are dead;
The wandering earth herself may be
Only a sudden flaming word,
In clanging space a moment heard,
Troubling the endless reverie.

Then nowise worship dusty deeds,
Nor seek, for this is also sooth,
To hunger fiercely after truth,
Lest all thy toiling only breeds
New dreams, new dreams; there is no truth
Saving in thine own heart. Seek, then,
No learning from the starry men,
Who follow with the optic glass
The whirling ways of stars that pass –
Seek, then, for this is also sooth,

No word of theirs – the cold star-bane
Has cloven and rent their hearts in twain,
And dead is all their human truth.
Go gather by the humming sea
Some twisted, echo-harbouring shell,
And to its lips thy story tell,
And they thy comforters will be,
Rewarding in melodious guile
Thy fretful words a little while,
Till they shall singing fade in ruth
And die a pearly brotherhood;
For words alone are certain good:
Sing, then, for this is also sooth.

I must be gone: there is a grave
Where daffodil and lily wave,
And I would please the hapless faun,
Buried under the sleepy ground,
With mirthful songs before the dawn.
His shouting days with mirth were crowned;
And still I dream he treads the lawn,
Walking ghostly in the dew,
Pierced by my glad singing through,
My songs of old earth's dreamy youth:
But ah! she dreams not now; dream thou!
For fair are poppies on the brow:
Dream, dream, for this is also sooth.

W. B. YEATS

The Lake Isle of Innisfree

I will arise and go now, and go to Innisfree,
And a small cabin build there, of clay and wattles made:
Nine bean-rows will I have there, a hive for the honey-bee,
And live alone in the bee-loud glade.

And I shall have some peace there, for peace comes
    dropping slow,
Dropping from the veils of the morning to where the
    cricket sings;
There midnight's all a glimmer, and noon a purple glow,
And evening full of the linnet's wings.

I will arise and go now, for always night and day
I hear lake water lapping with low sounds by the shore;
While I stand on the roadway, or on the pavements grey,
I hear it in the deep heart's core.

No Second Troy

Why should I blame her that she filled my days
With misery, or that she would of late
Have taught to ignorant men most violent ways,
Or hurled the little streets upon the great,
Had they but courage equal to desire?
What could have made her peaceful with a mind
That nobleness made simple as a fire,
With beauty like a tightened bow, a kind
That is not natural in an age like this,
Being high and solitary and most stern?
Why, what could she have done, being what she is?
Was there another Troy for her to burn?

The Second Coming

Turning and turning in the widening gyre
The falcon cannot hear the falconer;
Things fall apart; the centre cannot hold;
Mere anarchy is loosed upon the world,
The blood-dimmed tide is loosed, and everywhere
The ceremony of innocence is drowned;
The best lack all conviction, while the worst
Are full of passionate intensity.

Surely some revelation is at hand;
Surely the Second Coming is at hand.
The Second Coming! Hardly are those words out
When a vast image out of *Spiritus Mundi*
Troubles my sight: somewhere in sands of the desert
A shape with lion body and the head of a man,
A gaze blank and pitiless as the sun,
Is moving its slow thighs, while all about it
Reel shadows of the indignant desert birds.
The darkness drops again; but now I know
That twenty centuries of stony sleep
Were vexed to nightmare by a rocking cradle,
And what rough beast, its hour come round at last,
Slouches towards Bethlehem to be born?

PATRICK KAVANAGH

On Raglan Road

On Raglan Road on an autumn day I met her first and
    knew
That her dark hair would weave a snare that I might one
    day rue;
I saw the danger, yet I walked along the enchanted way,
And I said, let grief be a fallen leaf at the dawning of the
    day.

On Grafton Street in November we tripped lightly along
    the ledge
Of the deep ravine where can be seen the worth of
    passion's pledge,
The Queen of Hearts still making tarts and I not making
    hay—
O I loved too much and by such, by such, is happiness
    thrown away.

I gave her gifts of the mind, I gave her the secret sign that's
    known
To the artists who have known the true gods of sound and
    stone
And word and tint. I did not stint for I gave her poems to
    say
With her own name there and her own dark hair like
    clouds over fields of May.

On a quiet street where old ghosts meet I see her walking
    now
Away from me so hurriedly my reason must allow
That I had wooed not as I should a creature made of clay—
When the angel woos the clay he'd lose his wings at the
    dawn of day.

LOUIS MACNEICE

Snow

The room was suddenly rich and the great bay-window
    was
Spawning snow and pink roses against it
Soundlessly collateral and incompatible:
World is suddener than we fancy it.

World is crazier and more of it than we think,
Incorrigibly plural. I peel and portion
A tangerine and spit the pips and feel
The drunkenness of things being various.

And the fire flames with a bubbling sound for world
Is more spiteful and gay than one supposes—
On the tongue on the eyes on the ears on the palms of
    one's hands—
There is more than glass between the snow and the huge
    roses.

Punishment

I can feel the tug
of the halter at the nape
of her neck, the wind
on her naked front.

It blows her nipples
to amber beads,
it shakes the frail rigging
of her ribs.

I can see her drowned
body in the bog,
the weighing stone,
the floating rods and boughs.

Under which at first
she was a barked sapling
that is dug up
oak-bone, brain-firkin:

her shaved head
like a stubble of black corn,
her blindfold a soiled bandage,
her noose a ring

to store
the memories of love.
Little adulteress,
before they punished you

you were flaxen-haired,
undernourished, and your
tar-black face was beautiful.
My poor scapegoat,

I almost love you
but would have cast, I know,
the stones of silence.
I am the artful voyeur

of your brain's exposed
and darkened combs,
your muscles' webbing
and all your numbered bones:

I who have stood dumb
when your betraying sisters,
cauled in tar,
wept by the railings,

who would connive
in civilized outrage
yet understand the exact
and tribal, intimate revenge.

MICHAEL LONGLEY

Ceasefire

I

Put in mind of his own father and moved to tears
Achilles took him by the hand and pushed the old king
Gently away, but Priam curled up at his feet and
Wept with him until their sadness filled the building.

II

Taking Hector's corpse into his own hands Achilles
Made sure it was washed and, for the old king's sake,
Laid out in uniform, ready for Priam to carry
Wrapped like a present home to Troy at daybreak.

III

When they had eaten together, it pleased them both
To stare at each other's beauty as lovers might,
Achilles built like a god, Priam good-looking still
And full of conversation, who earlier had sighed:

IV

'I get down on my knees and do what must be done
And kiss Achilles' hand, the killer of my son.'

Wounds

Here are two pictures from my father's head –
I have kept them like secrets until now:
First, the Ulster Division at the Somme
Going over the top with 'Fuck the Pope!'
'No Surrender!': a boy about to die,
Screaming 'Give 'em one for the Shankill!'
'Wilder than Gurkhas' were my father's words
Of admiration and bewilderment.
Next comes the London-Scottish padre
Resettling kilts with his swagger-stick,
With a stylish backhand and a prayer.
Over a landscape of dead buttocks
My father followed him for fifty years.
At last, a belated casualty,
He said – lead traces flaring till they hurt –
'I am dying for King and Country, slowly.'
I touched his hand, his thin head I touched.

Now, with military honours of a kind,
With his badges, his medals like rainbows,
His spinning compass, I bury beside him
Three teenage soldiers, bellies full of
Bullets and Irish beer, their flies undone.
A packet of Woodbines I throw in,
A lucifer, the Sacred Heart of Jesus
Paralysed as heavy guns put out
The night-light in a nursery for ever;
Also a bus-conductor's uniform –
He collapsed beside his carpet-slippers
Without a murmur, shot through the head
By a shivering boy who wandered in

Before they could turn the television down
Or tidy away the supper dishes.
To the children, to a bewildered wife,
I think 'Sorry Missus' was what he said.

NUALA NÍ DHOMHNAILL
TRANSLATED BY PAUL MULDOON

The Language Issue

I place my hope in the water
in this little boat
of the language, the way a body might put
an infant

in a basket of intertwined
iris leaves,
its underside proofed
with bitumen and pitch,

then set the whole thing down amidst
the sedge
and bullrushes by the edge
of a river

only to have it borne hither and thither,
not knowing where it may end up;
in the lap, perhaps,
of some Pharaoh's daughter.

CIARAN CARSON

Belfast Confetti

Suddenly as the riot squad moved in, it was raining
    exclamation marks,
Nuts, bolts, nails, car-keys. A fount of broken type. And the
    explosion
Itself — an asterisk on the map. This hyphenated line, a burst
    of rapid fire . . .
I was trying to complete a sentence in my head, but it kept
    stuttering,
All the alleyways and side streets blocked with stops and
    colons.

I know this labyrinth so well — Balaklava, Raglan, Inkerman,
    Odessa Street —
Why can't I escape? Every move is punctuated. Crimea Street.
    Dead end again.
A Saracen, Kremlin-2 mesh. Makrolon face-shields. Walkie-
    talkies. What is
My name? Where am I coming from? Where am I going? A
    fusillade of question marks.

ROBERT BURNS

Ode to a Haggis

Fair fa' your honest, sonsie face,
Great Chieftain o' the Puddin-race!
Aboon them a' ye tak your place,
                Painch, tripe, or thairm:
Weel are ye wordy of a *grace*
                As lang's my arm.

The groaning trencher there ye fill,
Your hurdies like a distant hill,
Your *pin* wad help to mend a mill
                In time o' need,
While thro' your pores the dews distil
                Like amber bead.

His knife see rustic Labour dight,
An' cut you up wi' ready slight,
Trenching your gushing entrails bright,
                Like onie ditch;
And then, O what a glorious sight,
                Warm-reekin, rich!

Then, horn for horn, they stretch an' strive:
Deil tak the hindmost, on they drive,
Till a' their weel-swall'd kytes belyve
                Are bent like drums;
Then auld Guidman, maist like to rive,
                Bethankit hums.

Is there that owre his French *ragout*,
Or *olio* that wad staw a sow,
Or *fricassee* wad make her spew
                Wi' perfect sconner,
Looks down wi' sneering, scornfu' view
                On sic a dinner?

Poor devil! see him owre his trash,
As feckless as wither'd rash,
His spindle-shank, a guid whip-lash;
                His nieve a nit;
Thro' bloody flood or field to dash,
                O how unfit!

But mark the Rustic, *haggis-fed*,
The trembling earth resounds his tread,
Clap in his walie nieve a blade,
                He'll mak it whissle;
An' legs an' arms, an' heads will sned,
                Like taps o' thrissle.

Ye Pow'rs, wha mak mankind your care,
An' dish them out their bill o' fare,
Auld Scotland wants nae skinking ware
                That jaups in luggies;
But, if ye wish her gratefu' pray'r,
                Gie her a Haggis!

ROBERT BURNS

Mary Morison

O Mary, at thy window be!
    It is the wish'd, the trysted hour.
Those smiles and glances let me see,
    That makes the miser's treasure poor,
    How blithely wad I bide the stoure,
A weary slave frae sun to sun,
    Could I the rich reward secure –
The lovely Mary Morison.

Yestreen, when to the trembling string
    The dance gaed thro, the lighted ha',
To thee my fancy took its wing,
    I sat, but neither heard nor saw:
    Tho' this was fair, and that was braw,
And yon the toast of a' the town,
    I sigh'd, and said amang them a':–
'Ye are na Mary Morison.'

O Mary canst thou wreck his peace
    Wha for thy sake wad gladly die?
Or canst thou break that heart of his
    Whase only faut is loving thee?
    If love for love thou wilt na gie,
At least be pity to me shown:
    A thought ungentle canna be
The thought o' Mary Morison.

ROBERT BURNS

A Red, Red Rose

O my Luve is like a red, red rose
   That's newly sprung in June;
O my Luve is like the melody
   That's sweetly played in tune.

So fair art thou, my bonnie lass,
   So deep in luve am I;
And I will luve thee still, my dear,
   Till a' the seas gang dry.

Till a' the seas gang dry, my dear,
   And the rocks melt wi' the sun;
I will love thee still, my dear,
   While the sands o' life shall run.

And fare thee weel, my only luve!
   And fare thee weel awhile!
And I will come again, my luve,
   Though it were ten thousand mile.

ROBERT BURNS

A Man's a Man for A' That

Is there for honest poverty
　　That hings his head, an' a' that?
The coward slave, we pass him by –
　　We dare be poor for a' that!
For a' that, an' a' that!
　　Our toils obscure an' a' that,
The rank is but the guinea's stamp,
　　The man's the gowd for a' that.

What though on hamely fare we dine,
　　Wear hoddin grey, an' a' that?
Gie fools their silks, and knaves their wine –
　　A man's a man for a' that:
For a' that, and a' that,
　　Their tinsel show, an' a' that,
The honest man, tho' e'er sae poor,
　　Is king o' men for a' that.

Ye see yon birkie ca'd 'a lord',
　　Wha struts, an' stares, an' a' that?
Tho' hundreds worship at his word,
　　He's but a cuif for a' that,
For a' that, an' a' that,
　　His ribband, star, an' a' that,
The man o' independent mind,
　　He looks an' laughs at a' that.

A prince can mak a belted knight,
　　A marquis, duke, an' a' that!
But an honest man's aboon his might –
　　Guid faith, he mauna fa' that.
For a' that, an' a' that,

Their dignities, an' a' that,
The pith o' sense an' pride o' worth
  Are higher rank than a' that.

Then let us pray that come it may
  (As come it will for a' that,)
That Sense and Worth o'er a' the earth
  Shall bear the gree an' a' that!
For a' that, an' a' that,
  It's coming yet for a' that,
That man to man the world o'er
  Shall brothers be for a' that.

ROBERT BURNS

Ae Fond Kiss

Ae fond kiss, and then we sever;
Ae farewell and then forever!
Deep in heart-wrung tears I'll pledge thee,
Warring sighs and groans I'll wage thee.

Who shall say that fortune grieves him
While the star of hope she leaves him?
Me, nae chearfu' twinkle lights me;
Dark despair around benights me.

I'll ne'er blame my partial fancy,
Naething could resist my Nancy:
But to see her was to love her;
Love but her, and love for ever.

Had we never lov'd sae kindly,
Had we never lov'd sae blindly,
Never met – or never parted,
We had ne'er been broken-hearted.

Fare thee well, thou first and fairest!
Fare thee well, thou best and dearest!
Thine be ilka joy and treasure,
Peace, Enjoyment, Love and Pleasure!

Ae fond kiss, and then we sever;
Ae fareweel, Alas! for ever!
Deep in heart-wrung tears I'll pledge thee,
Warring sighs and groans I'll wage thee.

EDWIN MORGAN

King Billy

Grey over Riddrie the clouds piled up,
dragged their rain through the cemetery trees.
The gates shone cold. Wind rose
flaring the hissing leaves, the branches
swung, heavy, across the lamps.
Gravestones huddled in drizzling shadow,
flickering streetlight scanned the requiescats,
a name and an urn, a date, a dove
picked out, lost, half regained.
What is this dripping wreath, blown from its grave
red, white, blue, and gold
'To Our Leader of Thirty years Ago' –

Bareheaded, in dark suits, with flutes
and drums, they brought him here, in procession
seriously, King Billy of Brigton, dead,
from Bridgeton Cross; a memory of violence,
brooding days of empty bellies,
billiard smoke and a sour pint,
boots or fists, famous sherrickings,
the word, the scuffle, the flash, the shout,
bloody crumpling in the close,
bricks for papish windows, get
the Conks next time, the Conks ambush
the Billy Boys, the Billy Boys the Conks till
Sillitoe scuffs the razors down the stank –
No, but it isn't the violence they remember
but the legend of a violent man
born poor, gang-leader in the bad times
of idleness and boredom, lost in better days,
a bouncer in a betting club,
quiet man at last, dying

alone in Bridgeton in a box bed.
So a thousand people stopped the traffic
for the hearse of a folk hero and the flutes
threw 'Onward Christian Soldiers' to the winds
from unironic lips, the mourners kept
in step, and there were some who wept.

Go from the grave. The shrill flutes
are silent, the march dispersed.
Deplore what is to be deplored,
and then find out the rest.

HUGH MACDIARMID

from *A Drunk Man Looks at the Thistle*

The language that but sparely floo'ers
And maistly gangs to weed;
The thocht o' Christ and Calvary
Aye liddenin' in my heid;
And a' the dour provincial thocht
That merks the Scottish breed
– These are the thistle's characters,
To argie there's nae need.
Hoo weel my verse embodies
The thistle you can read!
– But will a Scotsman never
Frae this vile growth be freed? . . .

*   *   *

The thistle canna vanish quite.
Inside a' licht its shape maun glint,
A spirit wi' a skeleton in't.

The world, the flesh, 'll bide in us
As in the fire the unburnt buss,
Or as frae sire to son we gang
And coontless corpses in us thrang.

And e'en the glory that descends
I kenna whence on *me* depends.
And shapes itsel' to what is left
Whaur I o' me ha'e me bereft,
And still the form is mine, altho'
A force to which I ne'er could grow

Is movin' in't as 'twere a sea
That lang syne drooned the last o' me
– That drooned afore the warld began
A' that could ever come frae Man.

And as at sicna times am I,
I wad ha'e Scotland to my eye
Until I saw a timeless flame
Tak' Auchtermuchty for a name,
And kent that Ecclefechan stood
As part o' an eternal mood.

      *   *   *

The stars like thistle's roses floo'er
The sterile growth o' Space ootour,
That clad in bitter blasts spreids oot
Frae me, the sustenance o' its root.

O fain I'd keep my hert entire,
Fain hain the licht o' my desire,
But ech! the shinin' streams ascend,
And leave me empty at the end.

For aince it's toomed my hert and brain,
The thistle needs maun fa' again.
– But a' its growth 'll never fill
The hole it's turned my life intill! . . .

Yet ha'e I Silence left, the croon o' a'.

No' her, wha on the hills langsyne I saw
Liftin' a foreheid o' perpetual snaw.

No' her, wha in the how-dumb-deid o' nicht
Kyths, like Eternity in Time's despite.

No' her, withooten shape, wha's name is Daith,
No' Him, unkennable abies to faith

– God whom, gin e'er He saw a man, 'ud be
E'en mair dumfooner'd at the sicht than he

– But Him, whom nocht in man or Deity,
Or Daith or Dreid or Laneliness can touch,
Wha's deed owre often and has seen owre much.

O I ha'e Silence left,

        – 'And weel ye micht,'
Sae Jean'll say, 'efter sic a nicht!'

HUGH MACDIARMID

Scotland Small?

Scotland small? Our multiform, our infinite Scotland
    small?
Only as a patch of hillside may be a cliché corner
To a fool who cries 'Nothing but heather!' where in
    September another
Sitting there and resting and gazing round
Sees not only the heather but blaeberries
With bright green leaves and leaves already turned scarlet
Hiding ripe blue berries; and amongst the sage-green leaves
Of the bog-myrtle the golden flowers of the tormentil
    shining;
And on the small bare places, where the little Blackface
    sheep
Found grazing, milkworts blue as summer skies;
And down in neglected peat-hags, not worked
Within living memory, sphagnum moss in pastel shades
Of yellow, green, and pink; sundew and butterwort
Waiting with wide-open sticky leaves for their tiny winged
    prey;
And nodding harebells vying in their colour
With the blue butterflies that poise themselves delicately
    upon them;
And stunted rowans with harsh dry leaves of glorious
    colour.
'Nothing but heather!' – How marvellously descriptive!
    And incomplete!

TED HUGHES

The Warriors of the North

Bringing their frozen swords, their salt-bleached eyes,
   their salt-bleached hair,
The snow's stupefied anvils in rows,
Bringing their envy,
The slow ships feelered Southward, snails over the steep
   sheen of the water-globe.

Thawed at the red and black disgorging of abbeys,
The bountiful, cleft casks,
The fluttered bowels of the women of dead burghers,
And the elaborate, patient gold of the Gaels.

To no end
But this timely expenditure of themselves,
A cash-down, beforehand revenge, with extra,
For the gruelling relapse and prolongueur of their blood

Into the iron arteries of Calvin.

TED HUGHES

Heptonstall Old Church

A great bird landed here.

Its song drew men out of rock,
Living men out of bog and heather.

Its song put a light in the valleys
And harness on the long moors.

Its song brought crystal from space
And set it in men's heads.

Then the bird died.

Its giant bones
Blackened and became a mystery.

The crystal in men's heads
Blackened and fell to pieces.

The valleys went out
The moorland broke loose.

C. DAY LEWIS

'You that love England, who have an ear for her music'

You that love England, who have an ear for her music,
The slow movement of clouds in benediction,
Clear arias of light thrilling over her uplands,
Over the chords of summer sustained peacefully;
Ceaseless the leaves' counterpoint in a west wind lively,
Blossom and river rippling loveliest allegro,
And the storms of wood strings brass at year's finale:
Listen. Can you not hear the entrance of a new theme?

You who go out alone, on tandem or on pillion,
Down arterial roads riding in April,
Or sad beside lakes where hill-slopes are reflected
Making fires of leaves, your high hopes fallen:
Cyclists and hikers in company, day excursionists,
Refugees from cursed towns and devastated areas;
Know you seek a new world, a saviour to establish
Long-lost kinship and restore the blood's fulfilment.

You who like peace, good sticks, happy in a small way
Watching birds or playing cricket with schoolboys,
Who pay for drinks all round, whom disaster chose not;
Yet passing derelict mills and barns roof-rent
Where despair has burnt itself out—hearts at a
    standstill,
Who suffer loss, aware of lowered vitality;
We can tell you a secret, offer a tonic; only
Submit to the visiting angel, the strange new healer.

You above all who have come to the far end, victims
Of a run-down machine, who can bear it no longer;
Whether in easy chairs chafing at impotence
Or against hunger, bullies and spies preserving
The nerve for action, the spark of indignation—
Need fight in the dark no more, you know your
        enemies.
You shall be leaders when zero hour is signalled,
Wielders of power and welders of a new world.

MALORIE BLACKMAN

Searching for a Voice

'I have crossed an ocean
I have lost my tongue
from the root of the old one
a new one has sprung'

Grace Nichols, 'Epilogue'

WILLIAM BLAKE

London

I wander thro' each charter'd street,
Near where the charter'd Thames does flow.
And mark in every face I meet
Marks of weakness, marks of woe.

In every cry of every Man,
In every Infant's cry of fear,
In every voice: in every ban,
The mind-forg'd manacles I hear

How the Chimney-sweepers cry
Every blackning Church appalls,
And the hapless Soldiers sigh,
Runs in blood down Palace walls

But most thro' midnight streets I hear
How the youthful Harlots curse
Blasts the new-born Infants tear
And blights with plagues the Marriage hearse

WILLIAM BLAKE

Jerusalem

And did those feet in ancient time
Walk upon England's mountains green?
And was the holy Lamb of God
On England's pleasant pastures seen?

And did the Countenance Divine
Shine forth upon our clouded hills?
And was Jerusalem builded here
Among these dark Satanic Mills?

Bring me my bow of burning gold!
Bring me my arrows of desire!
Bring me my spear! O clouds, unfold!
Bring me my chariot of fire!

I will not cease from mental fight,
Nor shall my sword sleep in my hand,
Till we have built Jerusalem
In England's green and pleasant land.

WILLIAM BLAKE

A Poison Tree

I was angry with my friend:
I told my wrath, my wrath did end.
I was angry with my foe:
I told it not, my wrath did grow.

And I watered it in fears,
Night & morning with my tears:
And I sunned it with smiles.
And with soft deceitful wiles.

And it grew both day and night.
Till it bore an apple bright.
And my foe beheld it shine,
And he knew that it was mine.

And into my garden stole,
When the night had veild the pole;
In the morning glad I see;
My foe outstretched beneath the tree.

WILLIAM SHAKESPEARE

from *Othello* (Act V, Scene ii)

Enter Othello, with a light, Desdemona in her bed
OTHELLO:
   It is the cause, it is the cause, my soul:
   Let me not name it to you, you chaste stars!
   It is the cause. Yet I'll not shed her blood,
   Nor scar that whiter skin of hers than snow,
   And smooth as monumental alabaster:
   Yet she must die, else she'll betray more men.
   Put out the light, and then put out the light:
   If I quench thee, thou flaming minister,
   I can again thy former light restore,
   Should I repent me; but once put out thy light,
   Thou cunning'st pattern of excelling nature,
   I know not where is that Promethean heat
   That can thy light relume. When I have plucked thy rose,
   I cannot give it vital growth again,
   It needs must wither. I'll smell it on the tree.
      He kisses her
   O balmy breath, that dost almost persuade
   Justice to break her sword! One more, one more.
   Be thus when thou art dead and I will kill thee,
   And love thee after. One more, and this the last.
   So sweet was ne'er so fatal. I must weep.

JOHN MILTON

from *Paradise Lost*: Book I

Of man's first disobedience, and the fruit
Of that forbidden tree, whose mortal taste
Brought death into the world, and all our woe,
With loss of Eden, till one greater man
Restore us, and regain the blissful seat,
Sing Heav'nly Muse, that on the secret top
Of Oreb, or of Sinai, didst inspire
That shepherd, who first taught the chosen seed,
In the beginning how the heav'ns and earth
Rose out of Chaos: or if Sion hill
Delight thee more, and Siloa's brook that flowed
Fast by the oracle of God; I thence
Invoke thy aid to my advent'rous song,
That with no middle flight intends to soar
Above th' Aonian mount, while it pursues
Things unattempted yet in prose or rhyme.
And chiefly thou O Spirit, that dost prefer
Before all temples th' upright heart and pure,
Instruct me, for thou know'st; thou from the first
Wast present, and with mighty wings outspread
Dove-like sat'st brooding on the vast abyss
And mad'st it pregnant: what in me is dark
Illumine, what is low raise and support;
That to the heighth of this great argument
I may assert Eternal Providence,
And justify the ways of God to men.

from *Paradise Lost*: Book II

He ceased, and next him Moloch, sceptred king
Stood up, the strongest and the fiercest Spirit
That fought in Heav'n; now fiercer by despair:
His trust was with th' Eternal to be deemed
Equal in strength, and rather than be less
Cared not to be at all; with that care lost
Went all his fear: of God, or Hell, or worse
He recked not, and these words thereafter spake.
  My sentence is for open war: of wiles,
More unexpért, I boast not: them let those
Contrive who need, or when they need, not now.
For while they sit contriving, shall the rest,
Millions that stand in arms, and longing wait
The signal to ascend, sit ling'ring here
Heav'n's fugitives, and for their dwelling place
Accept this dark opprobrious den of shame,
The prison of his tyranny who reigns
By our delay? No, let us rather choose
Armed with Hell flames and fury all at once
O'er Heav'n's high tow'rs to force resistless way,
Turning our tortures into horrid arms
Against the Torturer; when to meet the noise
Of his almighty engine he shall hear
Infernal thunder, and for lightning see
Black fire and horror shot with equal rage
Among his angels; and his throne itself
Mixed with Tartarean sulphur, and strange fire,
His own invented torments. But perhaps
The way seems difficult and steep to scale
With upright wing against a higher foe.
Let such bethink them, if the sleepy drench
Of that forgetful lake benumb not still,

That in our proper motion we ascend
Up to our native seat: descent and fall
To us is adverse. Who but felt of late
When the fierce foe hung on our broken rear
Insulting, and pursued us through the deep,
With what compulsion and laborious flight
We sunk thus low? Th' ascent is easy then;
Th' event is feared; should we again provoke
Our stronger, some worse way his wrath may find
To our destruction: if there be in Hell
Fear to be worse destroyed: what can be worse
Than to dwell here, driv'n out from bliss, condemned
In this abhorrèd deep to utter woe;
Where pain of unextinguishable fire
Must exercise us without hope of end
The vassals of his anger, when the scourge
Inexorably, and the torturing hour
Calls us to penance? More destroyed than thus
We should be quite abolished and expire.
What fear we then? What doubt we to incense
His utmost ire? Which to the heighth enraged,
Will either quite consume us, and reduce
To nothing this essential, happier far
Than miserable to have eternal being:
Or if our substance be indeed divine,
And cannot cease to be, we are at worst
On this side nothing; and by proof we feel
Our power sufficient to disturb his Heav'n,
And with perpetual inroads to alarm,
Though inaccessible, his fatal throne:
Which if not victory is yet revenge.

EMILY DICKINSON

'From Cocoon forth a Butterfly'

From Cocoon forth a Butterfly
As Lady from her Door
Emerged – a Summer Afternoon –
Repairing Everywhere –

Without Design – that I could trace
Except to stray abroad
On Miscellaneous Enterprise
The Clovers – understood –

Her pretty Parasol be seen
Contracting in a Field
Where Men made Hay –
Then struggling hard
With an opposing Cloud –

Where Parties – Phantom as Herself –
To Nowhere – seemed to go
In purposeless Circumference –
As 'twere a Tropic Show –

And notwithstanding Bee – that worked –
And Flower – that zealous blew –
This Audience of Idleness
Disdained them, from the Sky –

Till Sundown crept – a steady Tide –
And Men that made the Hay –
And Afternoon – and Butterfly –
Extinguished – in the Sea –

EMILY DICKINSON

'"Hope" is the thing with feathers –'

"Hope" is the thing with feathers –
That perches in the soul –
And sings the tune without the words –
And never stops – at all –

And sweetest – in the Gale – is heard –
And sore must be the storm –
That could abash the little Bird
That kept so many warm –

I've heard it in the chillest land –
And on the strangest Sea –
Yet, never, in Extremity,
It asked a crumb – of Me.

EMILY DICKINSON

'Good Morning – Midnight –'

Good Morning – Midnight –
I'm coming Home –
Day – got tired of Me –
How could I – of Him?

Sunshine was a sweet place –
I liked to stay –
But Morn – didn't want me – now –
So – Goodnight – Day!

I can look – can't I –
When the East is Red?
The Hills – have a way – then –
That puts the Heart – abroad –

You – are not so fair – Midnight –
I chose – Day –
But – please take a little Girl –
He turned away!

EMILY DICKINSON

'*'Tis good – the looking back on Grief –*'

'Tis good – the looking back on Grief –
To re-endure a Day –
We thought the Mighty Funeral –
Of All Conceived Joy –

To recollect how Busy Grass
Did meddle – one by one –
Till all the Grief with Summer – waved
And none could see the stone.

And though the Woe you have Today
Be larger – As the Sea
Exceeds its Unremembered Drop –
They're Water – equally –

MAYA ANGELOU

Still I Rise

You may write me down in history
With your bitter, twisted lies,
You may trod me in the very dirt
But still, like dust, I'll rise.

Does my sassiness upset you?
Why are you beset with gloom?
'Cause I walk like I've got oil wells
Pumping in my living room.

Just like moons and like suns,
With the certainty of tides,
Just like hopes springing high,
Still I'll rise.

Did you want to see me broken?
Bowed head and lowered eyes?
Shoulders falling down like teardrops,
Weakened by my soulful cries?

Does my haughtiness offend you?
Don't you take it awful hard
'Cause I laugh like I've got gold mines
Diggin' in my own back yard.

You may shoot me with your words,
You may cut me with your eyes,
You may kill me with your hatefulness,
But still, like air, I'll rise.

Does my sexiness upset you?
Does it come as a surprise
That I dance like I've got diamonds
At the meeting of my thighs?

Out of the huts of history's shame
I rise
Up from a past that's rooted in pain
I rise
I'm a black ocean, leaping and wide,
Welling and swelling I bear in the tide.

Leaving behind nights of terror and fear
I rise
Into a daybreak that's wondrously clear
I rise
Bringing the gifts that my ancestors gave,
I am the dream and the hope of the slave.
I rise
I rise
I rise.

MAYA ANGELOU

Impeccable Conception

I met a Lady Poet
who took for inspiration
colored birds, and whispered words,
a lover's hesitation.

A falling leaf could stir her.
A wilting, dying rose
would make her write, both day and night,
the most rewarding prose.

She'd find a hidden meaning
in every pair of pants,
then hurry home to be alone
and write about romance.

JAMES BERRY

In Our Year 1941 My Letter to You Mother Africa

I sit
under the mango tree in our yard.
A woman passes along the village road,
loaded like a donkey.
I remember
I start my seventeenth year today
full of myself, but worried, and sad
remembering, you sold my ancestors
labelled, *not for human rights*,
And, O, your non-rights terms were
the fire of hell that stuck.
Mother Africa
my space walks your face
and am I condemned.
I refuse to grow up fixed here
going on with plantation lacks
and that lack of selfhood. Easily
I could grow up all drastic and extreme
and be wasted by law.
I want a university in me as I grow.

And now
three village men pass together,
each gripping his plantation machete.
I remember
we are stuck in time and hidden.
I refuse to be stuck in a maze
gripping a plantation machete.
I refuse to be Estate 'chop-bush' man
and a poverty path scarecrow.

Refuse to live in the terror of floods
and drought, and live left-out and moneyless.
I refuse to worry-worry Jesus Christ
with tear-faced complaints. And, O, I refuse
to walk my father's deadness,
Schooled to be wasted lawfully
and refuse it
I am doubly doomed to be wasted by law,
                              Mother Africa
New World offices and yards of rejection
threaten me, like every shack-dweller seared
by poverty and feels disgraced.
And people positioned to make changes
are not bothered how poverty sinks in.
Help stop my vexed feelings growing.
Help me have a university in me.

    And now
    a banana-truck passes.
            I remember
I dread that cap-in-hand
my father. His selfhood gutted –
all seasoned plantation corned-pork –
no education habit is there.
Not seeing his need and his rights
to make the world free,
not seeing the club of countries
that confiscated his ancestors' lives
still set boundaries, not seeing
no god for our good with us,
my father demands no more
than a small cut of land, hidden.
       Mother Africa
nobody at home here has any
education habit. Nobody stirs differently.
And I want life of the world in print.
I want to move about in all ages.
Not stay deformed, arrested, driven

by any drillmaster's voice telling
the growing good of myself is cancelled.
I want to be healed of smashed-up selfhood,
healed of the beating-up by bad-man history.
I want a university in me as a man.

     And now
     children pass by, going to loiter
     around the tourist beach.
           I remember
you were pillaged easily
and gutted easily. Existing dumb
you lost your continental wealth,
our inheritance, my inheritance.
And, a settled absence, you are a fixed
nonparticipator I never see. And while
others come and go from their motherlands,
I live marooned, renamed 'Negro'
meaning, of no origin,
not eligible for human rights.
           Mother Africa
I walk your face
and my heritage is pain.
And there somewhere
you make not one move.
Say nothing. Do nothing.
And I feel excessive doings could grip me.
I could call on bad doings as normal
and be wasted by law.
I want a university in me.

     And now
     at our gate, a village beggar stands
     calling my mother.
           I remember
I am third generation since slavery,
born into people stricken in traps,
Eight generations departed

with a last sigh, aware they leave
offsprings all heirs to losses,
to nothing, to a shame, and to faces
who meet enmity in the offices
of their land and the world.
You say nothing, do nothing
while your bosom's gold and gems are stars
in other people's days
around the world. And scattered
stubbornly, we are here
in the sun's comings and goings
anguished for our human status back.
                        Mother Africa
do you know, cruelties of your lacks
join forces with New World mangling?
Now I want to be healed.
I want university.

        And now
        village voices go by
        strong with the adjective 'black'
        in their curses.
                        I remember
in lessons at school you were degraded.
No village man accepts his photographs
that printed him truly black.
You never made a contact
never inspired me
never nurtured, counselled or consoled me.
I have never seen you, Africa,
never seen your sights or heard your sounds,
never heard your voice at home,
never understood one common
family thing about you beneath
one crinkly head or naked breast.
Any wonder I have no love for you?
Any wonder everybody at school despised you?
Tradition has it, our people's travel

to you does not happen. Visits
to a motherland are overlords' privilege.
What is your privilege?
                    Mother Africa
I want university.
Is there any help in you?
Will I have to store,
or bag-up and walk with, inherited hurt
and outrage of enslavement?
Will I transcend it?
Or will I grow up wasted
in deformity or being outlaw?

JAMES BERRY

On an Afternoon Train from Purley to Victoria, 1955

Hello, she said, and startled me.
Nice day. Nice day I agreed.
I am a Quaker she said and Sunday
I was moved in silence
to speak a poem loudly
for racial brotherhood.

I was thoughtful, then said
what poem came on like that?
One the moment inspired she said.
I was again thoughtful.

Inexplicably I saw
empty city streets lit dimly
in a day's first hours.
Alongside in darkness
was my father's big banana field.

Where are you from? she said.
Jamaica I said.
What part of Africa is Jamaica? she said.
Where Ireland is near Lapland I said.
Hard to see why you leave
such sunny country she said.
Snow falls elsewhere I said.
So sincere she was beautiful
as people sat down around us.

BENJAMIN ZEPHANIAH

Civil Lies

Dear Teacher,

When I was born in Ethiopia
Life began,
As I sailed down the Nile civilization began,
When I stopped to think universities were built,
When I set sail
Asians and true Americans sailed with me.

When we traded nations were built,
We did not have animals,
Animals lived with us,
We had so much time
Thirteen months made our year,
We created social services
And cities still stand.

So teacher do not say
Columbus discovered me
Check the great things I was doing
Before I suffered slavery.

Yours truly,

Mr Africa

BENJAMIN ZEPHANIAH

Walking Black Home

That day waz
A bad day,

I walked for
Many miles,

Unlike me,
I did not

Return any
Smiles.

Tired,

Weak
And
Hungry,

But I
Would not
Turn

Back,

Sometimes it's hard
To get a taxi
When you're Black.

BENJAMIN ZEPHANIAH

The British

Serves 60 million

Take some Picts, Celts and Silures
And let them settle,
Then overrun them with Roman conquerors.

Remove the Romans after approximately four hundred
    years
Add lots of Norman French to some
Angles, Saxons, Jutes and Vikings, then stir vigorously.

Mix some hot Chileans, cool Jamaicans, Dominicans,
Trinidadians and Bajans with some Ethiopians,
Chinese, Vietnamese and Sudanese.

Then take a blend of Somalians, Sri Lankans, Nigerians
And Pakistanis,
Combine with some Guyanese
And turn up the heat.

Sprinkle some fresh Indians, Malaysians, Bosnians,
Iraqis and Bangladeshis together with some
Afghans, Spanish, Turkish, Kurdish, Japanese
And Palestinians
Then add to the melting pot.

Leave the ingredients to simmer.

As they mix and blend allow their languages to flourish
Binding them together with English.

Allow time to be cool.

Add some unity, understanding, and respect for the future,
Serve with justice
And enjoy.

Note: All the ingredients are equally important. Treating one ingredient better than another will leave a bitter unpleasant taste.

Warning: An unequal spread of justice will damage the people and cause pain.

Give justice and equality to all.

Wherever I Hang

I leave me people, me land, me home
For reasons I not too sure
I forsake de sun
And de humming-bird splendour
Had big rats in de floorboard
So I pick up me new-world-self
And come to this place call England
At first I feeling like I in dream –
De misty greyness
I touching the walls to see if they real
They solid to de seam
And de people pouring from de underground system
Like beans
And when I look up to de sky
I see Lord Nelson high – too high to lie

And is so I sending home photos of myself
Among de pigeons and de snow
And is so I warding off de cold
And is so, little by little
I begin to change my calypso ways
Never visiting nobody
Before giving them clear warning
And waiting me turn in queue
Now, after all this time
I get accustom to de English life
But I still miss back-home side
To tell you de truth
I don't know really where I belaang

> Yes, divided to de ocean
> Divided to de bone

Wherever I hang me knickers – that's my home.

GRACE NICHOLS

Of Course When They Ask for Poems About the 'Realities' of Black Women

What they really want
at times
is a specimen
whose heart is in the dust

A mother-of-sufferer
trampled, oppressed
they want a little black blood
undressed
and validation
for the abused stereotype
already in their heads

Or else they want
a perfect song

I say I can write
no poem big enough
to hold the essence
        of a black woman
        or a white woman
        or a green woman

And there are black women
and black women
like a contrasting sky
of rainbow spectrum

Touch a black woman
you mistake for a rock
and feel her melting
down to fudge

Cradle a soft black woman
and burn fingers as you trace
revolution
beneath her woolly hair

And yes we cut bush
to clear paths
for our children
and yes,
we throw sprat
to catch whale
and yes,
if need be we'll trade
a piece-a-pussy
than see the pickney dem
in de grip-a-hungry-belly

Still, there ain't no
easy-belly category
    for a black woman
    or a white woman
    or a green woman

And there are black women
strong and eloquent
and focused

And there are black women
who somehow always manage to end up
frail victim

And there are black women
considered so dangerous
in South Africa
they prison them away

Maybe this poem is to say,
that I like to see
we black women
full-of-we-selves walking

Crushing out
with each dancing step
the twisted self-negating
history
we've inherited
    Crushing out
    with each dancing step.

JACKIE KAY

In my country

walking by the waters
down where an honest river
shakes hands with the sea,
a woman passed round me
in a slow, watchful circle,
as if I were a superstition;

or the worst dregs of her imagination,
so when she finally spoke
her words spliced into bars
of an old wheel. A segment of air.
Where do you come from?
'Here,' I said, 'Here. These parts.'

Her

I had been told about her.
How she would always, always.
How she would never, never.
I'd watched and listened
but I still fell for her,
how she always, always.
How she never, never.

In the small brave night,
her lips, butterfly moments.
I tried to catch her and she laughed,
a loud laugh that cracked me in two,
but then I had been told about her,
how she would always, always.
How she would never, never.

We two listened to the wind.
We two galloped a pace.
We two, up and away, away, away.
And now she's gone
like she said she would go.
But then I had been told about her –
how she would always, always.

LANGSTON HUGHES

The Weary Blues

Droning a drowsy syncopated tune,
Rocking back and forth to a mellow croon,
   I heard a Negro play.
Down on Lenox Avenue the other night
By the pale dull pallor of an old gas light
   He did a lazy sway. . . .
   He did a lazy sway. . . .
To the tune o' those Weary Blues.
With his ebony hands on each ivory key
He made that poor piano moan with melody.
   O Blues!
Swaying to and fro on his rickety stool
He played that sad raggy tune like a musical fool.
   Sweet Blues!
Coming from a black man's soul.
   O Blues!
In a deep song voice with a melancholy tone
I heard that Negro sing, that old piano moan—
   'Ain't got nobody in all this world,
   Ain't got nobody but ma self.
   I's gwine to quit ma frownin'
   And put ma troubles on the shelf.'
Thump, thump, thump, went his foot on the floor.
He played a few chords then he sang some more—
   'I got the Weary Blues
   And I can't be satisfied.
   Got the Weary Blues
   And can't be satisfied—
   I ain't happy no mo'
   And I wish that I had died.'

And far into the night he crooned that tune.
The stars went out and so did the moon.
The singer stopped playing and went to bed
While the Weary Blues echoed through his head.
He slept like a rock or a man that's dead.

LANGSTON HUGHES

The Negro Speaks of Rivers

(To W. E. B. Du Bois)

I've known rivers:
I've known rivers ancient as the world and older than the
   flow of human blood in human veins.
My soul has grown deep like the rivers.

I bathed in the Euphrates when dawns were young.
I built my hut near the Congo and it lulled me to sleep.
I looked upon the Nile and raised the pyramids above it.
I heard the singing of the Mississippi when Abe Lincoln
   went down to New Orleans, and I've seen its muddy
   bosom turn all golden in the sunset.

I've known rivers:
Ancient, dusky rivers.

My soul has grown deep like the rivers.

Song for a Dark Girl

Way Down South in Dixie
  (Break the heart of me)
They hung my black young lover
  To a cross roads tree.

Way Down South in Dixie
  (Bruised body high in air)
I asked the white Lord Jesus
  What was the use of prayer.

Way Down South in Dixie
  (Break the heart of me)
Love is a naked shadow
  On a gnarled and naked tree.

Harlem Sweeties

Have you dug the spill
Of Sugar Hill?
Cast your gims
On this sepia thrill:
Brown sugar lassie,
Caramel treat,
Honey-gold baby
Sweet enough to eat.
Peach-skinned girlie,
Coffee and cream,
Chocolate darling
Out of a dream.
Walnut tinted
Or cocoa brown,
Pomegranate-lipped
Pride of the town.
Rich cream-colored
To plum-tinted black,
Feminine sweetness
In Harlem's no lack.
Glow of the quince
To blush of the rose.
Persimmon bronze
To cinnamon toes.
Blackberry cordial,
Virginia Dare wine—
All those sweet colors
Flavor Harlem of mine!
Walnut or cocoa,
Let me repeat:
Caramel, brown sugar,
A chocolate treat.

Molasses taffy,
Coffee and cream,
Licorice, clove, cinnamon
To a honey-brown dream.
Ginger wine-gold,
Persimmon, blackberry,
All through the spectrum
Harlem girls vary—
So if you want to know beauty's
Rainbow-sweet thrill,
Stroll down luscious,
Delicious, *fine* Sugar Hill.

Theme for English B

The instructor said,

> *Go home and write*
> *a page tonight.*
> *And let that page come out of you—*
> *Then, it will be true.*

I wonder if it's that simple?
I am twenty-two, colored, born in Winston-Salem.
I went to school there, then Durham, then here
to this college on the hill above Harlem.
I am the only colored student in my class.
The steps from the hill lead down into Harlem,
through a park, then I cross St. Nicholas,
Eighth Avenue, Seventh, and I come to the Y,
the Harlem Branch Y, where I take the elevator
up to my room, sit down, and write this page:

It's not easy to know what is true for you or me
at twenty-two, my age. But I guess I'm what
I feel and see and hear, Harlem, I hear you:
hear you, hear me—we two—you, me, talk on this page.
(I hear New York, too.) Me—who?
Well, I like to eat, sleep, drink, and be in love.
I like to work, read, learn, and understand life.
I like a pipe for a Christmas present,
or records—Bessie, bop, or Bach.
I guess being colored doesn't make me *not* like
the same things other folks like who are other races.
So will my page be colored that I write?
Being me, it will not be white.
But it will be

a part of you, instructor.
You are white—
yet a part of me, as I am a part of you.
That's American.
Sometimes perhaps you don't want to be a part of me.
Nor do I often want to be a part of you.
But we are, that's true!
I guess you learn from me—
although you're older—and white—
and somewhat more free.

This is my page for English B.

LANGSTON HUGHES

Freedom

Freedom will not come
Today, this year
    Nor ever
Through compromise and fear.

I have as much right
As the other fellow has
    To stand
On my two feet
And own land.

I tire of hearing people say,
Let things take their course.
Tomorrow is another day.
I do not need freedom when I'm dead.
I cannot live on tomorrow's bread.
    Freedom
    Is a strong seed
    Planted
    In a great need.
    I live here, too.
    I want freedom
    Just as you.

Frederick Douglass: 1817–1895

Douglass was someone who,
Had he walked with wary foot
And frightened tread,
From very indecision
Might be dead,
Might have lost his soul,
But instead decided to be bold
And capture every street
On which he set his feet,
To route each path
Towards freedom's goal,
To make each highway
Choose *his* compass' choice,
To all the world cried,
Hear my voice! . . .
Oh, to be a beast, a bird,
Anything but a slave! he said.

Who would be free
Themselves must strike
The first blow, he said.

He died in 1895.
He is not dead.

ROY CAMPBELL

The Sisters

After hot loveless nights, when cold winds stream
Sprinkling the frost and dew, before the light,
Bored with the foolish things that girls must dream
Because their beds are empty of delight,

Two sisters rise and strip. Out from the night
Their horses run to their low-whistled pleas—
Vast phantom shapes with eyeballs rolling white
That sneeze a fiery steam about their knees:

Through the crisp manes their stealthy prowling hands,
Stronger than curbs, in slow caresses rove,
They gallop down across the milk-white sands
And wade far out into the sleeping cove:

The frost stings sweetly with a burning kiss
As intimate as love, as cold as death:
Their lips, whereon delicious tremors hiss,
Fume with the ghostly pollen of their breath.

Far out on the grey silence of the flood
They watch the dawn in smouldering gyres expand
Beyond them: and the day burns through their blood
Like a white candle through a shuttered hand.

ROY CAMPBELL

Choosing a Mast

This mast, new-shaved, through whom I rive the ropes,
Says she was once an oread of the slopes,
Graceful and tall upon the rocky highlands,
A slender tree as vertical as noon,
And her low voice was lovely as the silence
Through which a fountain whistles to the moon,
Who now of the white spray must take the veil
And, for her songs, the thunder of the sail.

I chose her for her fragrance, when the spring
With sweetest resins swelled her fourteenth ring
And with live amber welded her young thews:
I chose her for the glory of the Muse,
Smoother of forms, that her hard-knotted grain,
Grazed by the chisel, shaven by the plane,
Might from the steel as cool a burnish take
As from the bladed moon a windless lake.

I chose her for her eagerness of flight
Where she stood tiptoe on the rocky height
Lifted by her own perfume to the sun,
While through her rustling plumes with eager sound
Her eagle spirit, with the gale at one,
Spreading wide pinions, would have spurned the ground
And her own sleeping shadow, had they not
With thymy fragrance charmed her to the spot.

Lover of song, I chose this mountain pine
Not only for the straightness of her spine
But for her songs: for there she loved to sing
Through a long noon's repose of wave and wing,
The fluvial swirling of her scented hair
Sole rill of song in all that windless air,
And her slim form the naiad of the stream
Afloat upon the languor of its theme;

And for the soldier's fare on which she fed:
Her wine the azure, and the snow her bread;
And for her stormy watches on the height,
For only out of solitude or strife
Are born the sons of valour and delight;
And lastly for her rich, exulting life,
That with the wind stopped not its singing breath
But carolled on, the louder for its death.

Under a pine, when summer days were deep,
We loved the most to lie in love or sleep:
And when in long hexameters the west
Rolled his grey surge, the forest for his lyre,
It was the pines that sang us to our rest,
Loud in the wind and fragrant in the fire,
With legioned voices swelling all night long,
From Pelion to Provence, their storm of song.

It was the pines that fanned us in the heat,
The pines that cheered us in the time of sleet,
For which sweet gifts I set one dryad free;
No longer to the wind a rooted foe,
This nymph shall wander where she longs to be
And with the blue north wind arise and go,
A silver huntress with the moon to run
And fly through rainbows with the rising sun;

And when to pasture in the glittering shoals
The guardian mistral drives his thundering foals,
And when like Tartar horsemen racing free
We ride the snorting fillies of the sea,
My pine shall be the archer of the gale
While on the bending willow curves the sail
From whose great bow the long keel shooting home
Shall fly, the feathered arrow of the foam.

My People

my people
pass through gardens untouched by the toxic pollen of lilies
sway with the pre-factored rhythm of skyscrapers flexing in
    strong wind
thicken the air at night clubs and bus stops and cab ranks
    with their absence

my people
speak with the voices of ten million leaves, of earthquakes
    and dust motes
feed on starlight and moonshine and fallen crumbs of
    consumed dreams
grow with the vegetable fierceness of beansprouts, knowing
    that no growing is death

when they come
outracing planes whose snail trails silver the hollow sphere of
    the air
from earth where coal can burn twenty years in an
    underground seam
by sea, with sodium fire in their radiant lungfuls of water

their hands
will greet me with gestures that flux into silent legions of
    butterflies
will bear astounding weight with the sevenfold strength of
    ants
will move over me like perfect maggots purging the flesh of
    wounds

my people
are moving somewhere, trailing in wakes of their purpose the
     seasons
are wrung by an appetite gnawing at glaciers and atoms and
     bricks
are tirelessly looking for me, but in the wrong house, or
     country, or century

OGDEN NASH

The Cow

The cow is of the bovine ilk;
One end is moo, the other, milk.

Reflections on Ice-breaking

Candy
Is dandy
But liquor
Is quicker.

OGDEN NASH

Requiem

There was a young belle of old Natchez
Whose garments were always in patchez.
When comment arose
On the state of her clothes,
She drawled, When Ah itchez, Ah scratchez!

The Turtle

The turtle lives 'twixt plated decks
Which practically conceal its sex.
I think it clever of the turtle
In such a fix to be so fertile.

Arthur

There was an old man of Calcutta,
Who coated his tonsils with butta,
Thus converting his snore
From a thunderous roar
To a soft, oleaginous mutta.

LEWIS CARROLL

Jabberwocky

'Twas brillig, and the slithy toves
  Did gyre and gimble in the wabe;
All mimsy were the borogoves,
    And the mome raths outgrabe.

'Beware the Jabberwock, my son!
  The jaws that bite, the claws that catch!
Beware the Jubjub bird, and shun
    The frumious Bandersnatch!'

He took his vorpal sword in hand:
  Long time the manxome foe he sought –
So rested he by the Tumtum tree,
    And stood awhile in thought.

And as in uffish thought he stood,
  The Jabberwock, with eyes of flame,
Came whiffling through the tulgey wood,
    And burbled as it came!

One, two! One, two! And through and through
  The vorpal blade went snicker-snack!
He left it dead, and with its head
    He went galumphing back.

'And hast thou slain the Jabberwock?
   Come to my arms, my beamish boy!
O frabjous day! Callooh! Callay!'
      He chortled in his joy.

'Twas brillig, and the slithy toves
   Did gyre and gimble in the wabe;
All mimsy were the borogoves,
      And the mome raths outgrabe.

LEWIS CARROLL

The Mad Gardener's Song

He thought he saw an Elephant,
    That practised on a fife:
He looked again, and found it was
    A letter from his wife.
'At length I realise,' he said,
    'The bitterness of Life!'

He thought he saw a Buffalo
    Upon the chimney-piece:
He looked again, and found it was
    His Sister's Husband's Niece.
'Unless you leave this house,' he said,
    'I'll send for the Police!'

He thought he saw a Rattlesnake
    That questioned him in Greek:
He looked again, and found it was
    The Middle of Next Week.
'The only thing I regret,' he said,
    'Is that it cannot speak!'

He thought he saw a Banker's Clerk
    Descending from the bus:
He looked again, and found it was
    A Hippopotamus:
'If this should stay to dine,' he said,
    'There won't be much for us!'

He thought he saw a Kangaroo
  That worked a coffee-mill:
He looked again, and found it was
  A Vegetable-Pill.
'Were I to swallow this,' he said,
  'I should be very ill!'

He thought he saw a Coach-and-Four
  That stood beside his bed:
He looked again, and found it was
  A Bear without a Head.
'Poor thing,' he said, 'poor silly thing!
  It's waiting to be fed!'

He thought he saw an Albatross
  That fluttered round the lamp:
He looked again, and found it was
  A Penny-Postage-Stamp.
'You'd best be getting home,' he said:
  'The nights are very damp!'

He thought he saw a Garden-Door
  That opened with a key:
He looked again, and found it was
  A Double Rule of Three:
'And all its mystery,' he said,
  'Is clear as day to me!'

He thought he saw an Argument
  That proved he was the Pope:
He looked again, and found it was
  A Bar of Mottled Soap.
'A fact so dread,' he faintly said,
  'Extinguishes all hope!'

ROALD DAHL

'I've Eaten Many Strange and Scrumptious Dishes ...'

'I've eaten many strange and scrumptious dishes in my time,
Like jellied gnats and dandyprats and earwigs cooked in
    slime,
And mice with rice – they're really nice
When roasted in their prime.
(But don't forget to sprinkle them with just a pinch of grime.)

'I've eaten fresh mudburgers by the greatest cooks there are,
And scrambled dregs and stinkbugs' eggs and hornets stewed
    in tar,
And pails of snails and lizards' tails,
And beetles by the jar.
(A beetle is improved by just a splash of vinegar.)

'I often eat boiled slobbages. They're grand when served
    beside
Minced doodlebugs and curried slugs. And have you ever
    tried
Mosquitoes' toes and wampfish roes
Most delicately fried?
(The only trouble is they disagree with my inside.)

'I'm mad for crispy wasp-stings on a piece of buttered toast,
And pickled spines of porcupines. And then a gorgeous roast
Of dragon's flesh, well hung, not fresh –
It costs a pound at most,
(And comes to you in barrels if you order it by post.)

'I crave the tasty tentacles of octopi for tea
I like hot-dogs, I LOVE hot-frogs, and surely you'll agree

A plate of soil with engine oil's
A super recipe.
(I hardly need to mention that it's practically free.)

'For dinner on my birthday shall I tell you what I chose:
Hot noodles made from poodles on a slice of garden hose –
And a rather smelly jelly
Made of armadillo's toes.
(The jelly is delicious, but you have to hold your nose.)

'Now comes,' *the Centipede declared*, 'the burden of my
    speech:
These foods are rare beyond compare – some are right out of
    reach;
But there's no doubt I'd go without
A million plates of each
For one small mite,
One tiny bite
Of this FANTASTIC PEACH!'

EDWARD GOREY

There's a Rather Odd Couple in Herts

There's a rather odd couple in Herts
Who are cousins (or so each asserts);
    Their sex is in doubt
    For they're never without
Their moustaches and long, trailing skirts.

From Number Nine, Penwiper Mews

From Number Nine, Penwiper Mews,
There is really abominable news:
    They've discovered a head
    In the box for the bread,
But nobody seems to know whose.

The Elephant or, The Force of Habit

A tail behind, a trunk in front,
Complete the usual elephant.
The tail in front, the trunk behind
Is what you very seldom find.

If you for specimens should hunt
With trunks behind and tails in front,
That hunt would occupy you long;
The force of habit is so strong.

from *The Crocodile or, Public Decency*

Though some at my aversion smile,
I cannot love the crocodile.
Its conduct does not seem to me
Consistent with sincerity.

Where Nile, with beneficial flood,
Improves the desert sand to mud,
The infant child, its banks upon,
Will run about with nothing on.
The London County Council not
Being adjacent to the spot,
This is the consequence. Meanwhile,
What is that object in the Nile
Which swallows water, chokes and spits?
It is the crocodile in fits.

'Oh infant! oh my country's shame!
Suppose a European came!
Picture his feelings, on his pure
Personally conducted tour!
The British Peer's averted look,
The mantling blush of Messrs Cook!
Come, awful infant, come and be
Dressed, if in nothing else, in me.'

Then disappears into the Nile
The infant, clad in crocodile,
And meekly yields his youthful breath
To darkness, decency, and death.
His mother, in the local dells,
Deplores him with Egyptian yells:

Her hieroglyphic howls are vain,
Nor will the lost return again.
The crocodile itself no less
Displays, but does not feel, distress,

And with its tears augments the Nile;
The false, amphibious crocodile.

The Owl and the Pussy-Cat

[I]

The Owl and the Pussy-cat went to sea
  In a beautiful pea-green boat,
They took some honey, and plenty of money,
  Wrapped up in a five-pound note.
The Owl looked up to the stars above,
  And sang to a small guitar,
'O lovely Pussy! O Pussy, my love,
    What a beautiful Pussy you are,
      You are,
      You are!
  What a beautiful Pussy you are!'

[II]

Pussy said to the Owl, 'You elegant fowl!
  How charmingly sweet you sing!
O let us be married! too long we have tarried:
  But what shall we do for a ring?'
They sailed away, for a year and a day,
  To the land where the Bong-tree grows
And there in a wood a Piggy-wig stood
    With a ring at the end of his nose,
      His nose,
      His nose,
  With a ring at the end of his nose.

[III]

'Dear Pig, are you willing to sell for one shilling
  Your ring?' Said the Piggy, 'I will.'
So they took it away, and were married next day
  By the Turkey who lives on the hill.
They dined on mince, and slices of quince,

Which they ate with a runcible spoon;
And hand in hand, on the edge of the sand,
They danced by the light of the moon,
The moon,
The moon,
They danced by the light of the moon.

RICHARD EDWARDS

Stevie Scared

Stevie Scared, scared of the dark,
Scared of rats, of dogs that bark,
Scared of his fat dad, scared of his mother,
Scared of his sis and his tattooed brother,
Scared of tall girls, scared of boys,
Scared of ghosts and sudden noise,
Scared of spiders, scared of bees,
Scared of standing under trees,
Scared of shadows, scared of adders,
Scared of the devil, scared of ladders,
Scared of the hailstones, scared of rain,
Scared of falling down the drain,
Stevie Scared, scared of showing
He's so scared and people knowing,
Spends his whole time kicking, fighting,
Shoving, pinching, butting, biting,
Bashing little kids about
(Just in case they find him out).

HILAIRE BELLOC

Matilda (Who Told Lies, and Was Burned to Death)

Matilda told such Dreadful Lies,
It made one Gasp and Stretch one's Eyes;
Her Aunt, who, from her Earliest Youth,
Had kept a Strict Regard for Truth,
Attempted to Believe Matilda:
The effort very nearly killed her,
And would have done so, had not She
Discovered this Infirmity.
For once, towards the Close of Day,
Matilda, growing tired of play,
And finding she was left alone,
Went tiptoe to the Telephone
And summoned the Immediate Aid
Of London's Noble Fire-Brigade.
Within an hour the Gallant Band
Were pouring in on every hand,
From Putney, Hackney Downs, and Bow
With Courage high and Hearts a-glow
They galloped, roaring through the Town,
'Matilda's House is Burning Down!'
Inspired by British Cheers and Loud
Proceeding from the Frenzied Crowd,
They ran their ladders through a score
Of windows on the Ball Room Floor;
And took Peculiar Pains to Souse
The Pictures up and down the House,
Until Matilda's Aunt succeeded
In showing them they were not needed;
And even then she had to pay
To get the Men to go away!

It happened that a few Weeks later
Her Aunt was off to the Theatre
To see that Interesting Play
The Second Mrs Tanqueray.
She had refused to take her Niece
To hear this Entertaining Piece:
A Deprivation Just and Wise
To punish her for Telling Lies.
That Night a Fire *did* break out –
You should have heard Matilda Shout!
You should have heard her Scream and Bawl,
And throw the window up and call
To People passing in the Street –
(The rapidly increasing Heat
Encouraging her to obtain
Their confidence) – but all in vain!
For every time She shouted 'Fire!'
They only answered 'Little Liar'!
And therefore when her Aunt returned,
Matilda, and the House, were Burned.

SHEILA HANCOCK

Love and Loss

'And did you get what
you wanted from this life, even so?
I did.
And what did you want?
To call myself beloved, to feel myself
beloved on the earth.'

Raymond Carver, 'Late Fragment'

RAYMOND CARVER

Late Fragment

And did you get what
you wanted from this life, even so?
I did.
And what did you want?
To call myself beloved, to feel myself
beloved on the earth.

The Ivy Crown

The whole process is a lie,
        unless,
                crowned by excess,
it break forcefully,
        one way or another,
                from its confinement—
or find a deeper well.
        Antony and Cleopatra
                were right;
they have shown
        the way. I love you
                or I do not live
at all.

Daffodil time
        is past. This is
                summer, summer!
the heart says,
        and not even the full of it.
                No doubts
are permitted—
        though they will come
                and may
before our time
        overwhelm us.
                We are only mortal
but being mortal
        can defy our fate.
                We may
by an outside chance
        even win! We do not
                look to see

jonquils and violets
                come again
                        but there are,
still,
            the roses!

Romance has no part in it.
                The business of love is
                        cruelty *which*,
by our wills,
                we transform
                        to live together.
It has its seasons,
                for and against,
                        whatever the heart
fumbles in the dark
                to assert
                        toward the end of May.
Just as the nature of briars
                is to tear flesh,
                        I have proceeded
through them.
                Keep
                        the briars out,
they say.
                You cannot live
                        and keep free of
briars.

Children pick flowers.
                Let them.
                        Though having them
in hand
                they have no further use for them
                        but leave them crumpled
at the curb's edge.

At our age the imagination
                across the sorry facts
                                lifts us
to make roses
                stand before thorns.
                                Sure
love is cruel
                and selfish
                                and totally obtuse—
at least, blinded by the light,
                young love is.
                                But we are older,
I to love
                and you to be loved,
                                we have,
no matter how,
                by our wills survived
                                to keep
the jeweled prize
                always
                                at our finger tips.
We will it so
                and so it is
                                past all accident.

W. H. AUDEN

Lullaby

Lay your sleeping head, my love,
Human on my faithless arm;
Time and fevers burn away
Individual beauty from
Thoughtful children, and the grave
Proves the child ephemeral:
But in my arms till break of day
Let the living creature lie,
Mortal, guilty, but to me
The entirely beautiful.

Soul and body have no bounds:
To lovers as they lie upon
Her tolerant enchanted slope
In their ordinary swoon,
Grave the vision Venus sends
Of supernatural sympathy,
Universal love and hope;
While an abstract insight wakes
Among the glaciers and the rocks
The hermit's carnal ecstasy.

Certainty, fidelity
On the stroke of midnight pass
Like vibrations of a bell
And fashionable madmen raise
Their pedantic boring cry:
Every farthing of the cost,
All the dreaded cards foretell,
Shall be paid, but from this night
Not a whisper, not a thought,
Not a kiss nor look be lost.

Beauty, midnight, vision dies:
Let the winds of dawn that blow
Softly round your dreaming head
Such a day of welcome show
Eye and knocking heart may bless,
Find our mortal world enough;
Noons of dryness find you fed
By the involuntary powers,
Nights of insult let you pass
Watched by every human love.

W. H. AUDEN

Stop All the Clocks

Stop all the clocks, cut off the telephone,
Prevent the dog from barking with a juicy bone,
Silence the pianos and with muffled drum
Bring out the coffin, let the mourners come.

Let aeroplanes circle moaning overhead
Scribbling on the sky the message He Is Dead,
Put crêpe bows round the white necks of the public doves,
Let the traffic policemen wear black cotton gloves.

He was my North, my South, my East and West,
My working week and my Sunday rest,
My noon, my midnight, my talk, my song;
I thought that love would last for ever: I was wrong.

The stars are not wanted now: put out every one;
Pack up the moon and dismantle the sun;
Pour away the ocean and sweep up the wood.
For nothing now can ever come to any good.

Love (III)

Love bade me welcome; yet my soul drew back,
　　Guilty of dust and sin.
But quick-eyed Love, observing me grow slack
　　From my first entrance in,
Drew nearer to me, sweetly questioning
　　If I lack'd anything.

'A guest,' I answer'd, 'worthy to be here:'
　　Love said, 'You shall be he.'
'I, the unkind, ungrateful? Ah, my dear,
　　I cannot look on thee.'
Love took my hand and smiling did reply,
　　'Who made the eyes but I?'

'Truth, Lord, but I have marr'd them: let my shame
　　Go where it doth deserve.'
'And know you not,' says Love, 'Who bore the
　　　　blame?'
　　'My dear, then I will serve.'
'You must sit down,' says Love, 'and taste my meat.'
　　So I did sit and eat.

ARTHUR HUGH CLOUGH

Put Forth Thy Leaf

Put forth thy leaf, thou lofty plane,
  East winds and frost are safely gone;
With zephyr mild and balmy rain
  The summer comes serenely on;
Earth, air, and sun and skies combine
  To promise all that's kind and fair:—
But thou, O human heart of mine,
  Be still, contain thyself, and bear.

December days were brief and chill,
  The winds of March were wild and drear,
And, nearing and receding still,
  Spring never would, we thought, be here.
The leaves that burst, the suns that shine,
  Had, not the less, their certain date:—
And thou, O human heart of mine,
  Be still, refrain thyself, and wait.

ARTHUR HUGH CLOUGH

Not in Vain

Say not the struggle nought availeth,
　The labour and the wounds are vain,
The enemy faints not, nor faileth,
　And as things have been they remain.

If hopes were dupes, fears may be liars;
　It may be, in yon smoke concealed,
Your comrades chase e'en now the fliers,
　And, but for you, possess the field.

For while the tired waves, vainly breaking,
　Seem here no painful inch to gain,
Far back, through creeks and inlets making,
　Comes silent, flooding in, the main.

And not by eastern windows only,
　When daylight comes, comes in the light,
In front, the sun climbs slow, how slowly,
　But westward, look, the land is bright.

DANTE GABRIEL ROSSETTI

The One Hope

When vain desire at last and vain regret
   Go hand in hand to death, and all is vain,
   What shall assuage the unforgotten pain
And teach the unforgetful to forget?
Shall Peace be still a sunk stream long unmet,—
   Or may the soul at once in a green plain
   Stoop through the spray of some sweet life-fountain
And cull the dew-drenched flowering amulet?

Ah! when the wan soul in that golden air
   Between the scriptured petals softly blown
   Peers breathless for the gift of grace unknown,—
Ah! let none other written spell soe'er,
But only the one Hope's one name be there,—
   Not less nor more, but even that word alone.

ELIZABETH BARRETT BROWNING

Loved Once

    I classed, appraising once
Earth's lamentable sounds, the 'well-a-day,'
The jarring 'yea' and 'nay,'
The fall of kisses on unanswering clay,
The sobbed 'farewell,' the 'welcome' mournfuller,—
But all did leaven the air
With a less bitter leaven of sure despair
    Than these words—'I loved once.'

    And who saith, 'I loved once'?
Not angels, whose clear eyes love, love foresee,
Love through eternity!
And by To Love, do apprehend To Be.
Not God, called Love, his noble crown-name, casting
A light too broad for blasting!
The great God, changing not from everlasting,
    Saith never, 'I loved once.'

    Oh! never is 'loved once'
Thy word, thou Victim-Christ, misprizèd Friend!
Thy cross and curse may rend;
But, having loved, Thou lovest to the end!
This is man's saying—man's!—too weak to move
One spherèd star above,
Man desecrates the eternal God-word, Love,
    By his 'no more' and 'once.'

    How say ye 'We loved once,'
Blasphemers! Is your earth not cold enow,
Mourners, without that snow?
Ah, friends! and would ye wrong each other so?

And could ye say of some, whose love is known,
Whose prayers have met your own,
Whose tears have fallen for you, whose smiles have
        shone
    So long, 'We loved them once'?

        Could ye, 'We loved her once,'
Say calm of me, sweet friends, when out of sight—
When hearts of better right
Stand in between me and your happy light;
Or when, as flowers kept too long in the shade,
Ye find my colours fade,
And all that is not love in me decayed—
    Such words, 'We loved me once'?

        Could ye, 'We loved her once,'
Say cold of me, when further put away
In earth's sepulchral clay—
When mute the lips which deprecate to-day?
Not so: not then—least then—when life is shriven,
And death's full joy is given,
Of those who sit and love you up in heaven,
    Say not, 'We loved them once!'

        Say never, ye loved once!
God is too near above, the grave beneath,
And all our moments breathe
Too quick in mysteries of life and death,
For such a word. The eternities avenge
Affections light of range;
There comes no change to justify that change,
    Whatever comes—loved once!

        And yet that same word—'once'—
Is humanly acceptive! Kings have said,
Shaking a discrowned head,
'We ruled once;'—dotards, 'We once taught and led;'

Cripples 'once' danced i'the vines; and bards approved
Were once by scornings moved;
But love strikes one hour—Love. Those never loved
    Who dream that they loved once.

ELIZABETH BARRETT BROWNING

Comfort

Speak low to me, my Saviour, low and sweet
From out the hallelujahs, sweet and low,
Lest I should fear and fall, and miss Thee so
Who art not missed by any that entreat.
Speak to me as to Mary at thy feet!
And if no precious gums my hands bestow,
Let my tears drop like amber while I go
In reach of thy divinest voice complete
In humanest affection—thus, in sooth,
To lose the sense of losing. As a child,
Whose song-bird seeks the wood for evermore,
Is sung to in its stead by mother's mouth
Till, sinking on her breast, love-reconciled,
He sleeps the faster that he wept before.

ELIZABETH BARRETT BROWNING

Irreparableness

I have been in the meadows all the day
And gathered there the nosegay that you see,
Singing within myself as bird or bee,
When such do field-work on a morn of May.
But, now I look upon my flowers, decay
Has met them in my hands more fatally
Because more warmly clasped—and sobs are free
To come instead of songs. What do you say,
Sweet counsellors, dear friends? that I should go
Back straightway to the fields and gather more?
Another, sooth, may do it, but not I!
My heart is very tired, my strength is low,
My hands are full of blossoms plucked before,
Held dead within them till myself shall die.

ELIZABETH BARRETT BROWNING

Sonnets from the Portuguese

How do I love thee? Let me count the ways.
I love thee to the depth and breadth and height
My soul can reach, when feeling out of sight
For the ends of Being and ideal Grace.
I love thee to the level of everyday's
Most quiet need, by sun and candlelight.
I love thee freely, as men strive for Right;
I love thee purely, as they turn from Praise.
I love thee with the passion put to use
In my old griefs, and with my childhood's faith.
I love thee with a love I seemed to lose
With my lost saints, – I love thee with the breath,
Smiles, tears, of all my life! – and, if God choose,
I shall but love thee better after death.

ELIZABETH BARRETT BROWNING

Grief

I tell you, hopeless grief is passionless;
That only men incredulous of despair,
Half-taught in anguish, through the midnight air
Beat upward to God's throne in loud access
Of shrieking and reproach. Full desertness,
In souls as countries, lieth silent-bare
Under the blanching, vertical eye-glare
Of the absolute Heavens. Deep-hearted man, express
Grief for thy Dead in silence like to death –
Most like a monumental statue set
In everlasting watch and moveless woe
Till itself crumble to the dust beneath.
Touch it; the marble eyelids are not wet:
If it could weep, it could arise and go.

Enosis

Thought is deeper than all speech,
  Feeling deeper than all thought;
Souls to souls can never teach
  What unto themselves was taught.

We are spirits clad in veils;
  Man by man was never seen;
All our deep communing fails
  To remove the shadowy screen.

Heart to heart was never known;
  Mind with mind did never meet;
We are columns, left alone,
  Of a temple once complete.

Like the stars that gem the sky,
  Far apart, though seeming near,
In our light we scattered lie;
  All is thus but starlight here.

What is social company
  But a babbling summer stream?
What our wise philosophy
  But the glancing of a dream?

Only when the sun of love
  Melts the scattered stars of thought;
Only when we live above
  What the dim-eyed world hath taught;

Only when our souls are fed
    By the Fount which gave them birth,
And by inspiration led
    Which they never drew from earth;

We, like parted drops of rain,
    Swelling till they melt and run,
Shall be all absorbed again,
    Melting, flowing into one.

WILLIAM WORDSWORTH

Desideria

Surprised by joy—impatient as the wind
I turned to share the transport—Oh! with whom
But Thee, deep buried in the silent tomb,
That spot which no vicissitude can find?
Love, faithful love, recalled thee to my mind—
But how could I forget thee? Through what power,
Even for the least division of an hour,
Have I been so beguiled as to be blind
To my most grievous loss?—That thought's return
Was the worst pang that sorrow ever bore,
Save one, one only, when I stood forlorn,
Knowing my heart's best treasure was no more;
That neither present time, nor years unborn,
Could to my sight that heavenly face restore.

ADAM ZAGAJEWSKI
(translated by Clare Cavanagh)

Try to Praise the Mutilated World

Try to praise the mutilated world.
Remember June's long days,
and wild strawberries, drops of wine, the dew.
The nettles that methodically overgrow
the abandoned homesteads of exiles.
You must praise the mutilated world.
You watched the stylish yachts and ships;
one of them had a long trip ahead of it,
while salty oblivion awaited others.
You've seen the refugees heading nowhere,
you've heard the executioners sing joyfully.
You should praise the mutilated world.
Remember the moments when we were together
in a white room and the curtain fluttered.
Return in thought to the concert where music flared.
You gathered acorns in the park in autumn
and leaves eddied over the earth's scars.
Praise the mutilated world
and the grey feather a thrush lost,
and the gentle light that strays and vanishes
and returns.

MATTHEW ARNOLD

Growing Old

What is it to grow old?
Is it to lose the glory of the form,
The lustre of the eye?
Is it for beauty to forego her wreath?
– Yes, but not this alone.

Is it to feel our strength –
Not our bloom only, but our strength – decay?
Is it to feel each limb
Grow stiffer, every function less exact,
Each nerve more loosely strung?

Yes, this, and more; but not
Ah, 'tis not what in youth we dream'd 'twould be!
'Tis not to have our life
Mellow'd and soften'd as with sunset-glow,
A golden day's decline.

'Tis not to see the world
As from a height, with rapt prophetic eyes,
And heart profoundly stirr'd;
And weep, and feel the fulness of the past,
The years that are no more.

It is to spend long days
And not once feel that we were ever young;
It is to add, immured
In the hot prison of the present, month
To month with weary pain.

It is to suffer this,
And feel but half, and feebly, what we feel.
Deep in our hidden heart
Festers the dull remembrance of a change,
But no emotion – none.

It is – last stage of all –
When we are frozen up within, and quite
The phantom of ourselves,
To hear the world applaud the hollow ghost
Which blamed the living man.

EDNA ST VINCENT MILLAY

'As to some lovely temple, tenantless'

As to some lovely temple, tenantless
Long since, that once was sweet with shivering brass,
Knowing well its altars ruined and the grass
Grown up between the stones, yet from excess
Of grief hard driven, or great loneliness,
The worshiper returns, and those who pass
Marvel him crying on a name that was,—
So is it now with me in my distress.
Your body was a temple to Delight;
Cold are its ashes whence the breath is fled,
Yet here one time your spirit was wont to move;
Here might I hope to find you day or night,
And here I come to look for you, my love,
Even now, foolishly, knowing you are dead.

EDNA ST VINCENT MILLAY

'Time does not bring relief; you all have lied'

Time does not bring relief; you all have lied
Who told me time would ease me of my pain!
I miss him in the weeping of the rain;
I want him at the shrinking of the tide;
The old snows melt from every mountain-side,
And last year's leaves are smoke in every lane;
But last year's bitter loving must remain
Heaped on my heart, and my old thoughts abide.
There are a hundred places where I fear
To go,—so with his memory they brim.
And entering with relief some quiet place
Where never fell his foot or shone his face
I say, "There is no memory of him here!"
And so stand stricken, so remembering him.

EDNA ST VINCENT MILLAY

Dirge Without Music

I am not resigned to the shutting away of loving hearts in
  the hard ground.
So it is, and so it will be, for so it has been, time out of mind:
Into the darkness they go, the wise and the lovely. Crowned
With lilies and with laurel they go; but I am not resigned.

Lovers and thinkers, into the earth with you.
Be one with the dull, the indiscriminate dust.
A fragment of what you felt, of what you knew,
A formula, a phrase remains, – but the best is lost.

The answers quick and keen, the honest look, the laughter,
  the love, –
They are gone. They are gone to feed the roses. Elegant
  and curled
Is the blossom. Fragrant is the blossom. I know. But I do
  not approve.
More precious was the light in your eyes than all the roses
  in the world.

Down, down, down into the darkness of the grave
Gently they go, the beautiful, the tender, the kind;
Quietly they go, the intelligent, the witty, the brave.
I know. But I do not approve. And I am not resigned.

W. B. YEATS

When You Are Old

When you are old and grey and full of sleep,
And nodding by the fire, take down this book,
And slowly read, and dream of the soft look
Your eyes had once, and of their shadows deep;

How many loved your moments of glad grace,
And loved your beauty with love false or true,
But one man loved the pilgrim soul in you,
And loved the sorrows of your changing face;

And bending down beside the glowing bars,
Murmur, a little sadly, how Love fled
And paced upon the mountains overhead
And hid his face amid a crowd of stars.

ROBERT FROST

The Oven Bird

There is a singer everyone has heard,
Loud, a mid-summer and a mid-wood bird,
Who makes the solid tree trunks sound again.
He says that leaves are old and that for flowers
Mid-summer is to spring as one to ten.
He says the early petal-fall is past
When pear and cherry bloom went down in showers
On sunny days a moment overcast;
And comes that other fall we name the fall.
He says the highway dust is over all.
The bird would cease and be as other birds
But that he knows in singing not to sing.
The question that he frames in all but words
Is what to make of a diminished thing.

PHILIP LARKIN

Mother, Summer, I

My mother, who hates thunder storms,
Holds up each summer day and shakes
It out suspiciously, lest swarms
Of grape-dark clouds are lurking there;
But when the August weather breaks
And rains begin, and brittle frost
Sharpens the bird-abandoned air,
Her worried summer look is lost,

And I her son, though summer-born
And summer-loving, none the less
Am easier when the leaves are gone
Too often summer days appear
Emblems of perfect happiness
I can't confront: I must await
A time less bold, less rich, less clear:
An autumn more appropriate.

PHILIP LARKIN

The Mower

The mower stalled, twice; kneeling, I found
A hedgehog jammed up against the blades,
Killed. It had been in the long grass.

I had seen it before, and even fed it, once.
Now I had mauled its unobtrusive world
Unmendably. Burial was no help:

Next morning I got up and it did not.
The first day after a death, the new absence
Is always the same; we should be careful

Of each other, we should be kind
While there is still time.

Break, Break, Break

Break, break, break,
   On thy cold gray stones, O Sea!
And I would that my tongue could utter
   The thoughts that arise in me.

O well for the fisherman's boy,
   That he shouts with his sister at play!
O well for the sailor lad,
   That he sings in his boat on the bay!

And the stately ships go on
   To their haven under the hill!
But O for the touch of a vanish'd hand,
   And the sound of a voice that is still!

Break, break, break,
   At the foot of thy crags, O Sea!
But the tender grace of a day that is dead
   Will never come back to me.

BRIAN PATTEN

So Many Different Lengths of Time

Cuánto vive el hombre, por fin? Vive mil días o uno solo?
Una semana o varios siglos? Por cuánto tiempo muere el hombre?
Qué quiere decir 'para siempre'?
Preocupado por este asunto me dediqué a aclarar las cosas.

– PABLO NERUDA

How long is a man's life, finally?
A thousand days, or only one?
One week, or a few centuries?
How long does a man's death last?
And what do we mean when we say, 'gone forever'?

Adrift in such preoccupations, we seek clarification.
We can go to the philosophers,
but they will grow tired of our questions.
We can go to the priests and the rabbis
but they might be busy with administrations.

*   *   *

So, how long does a man live, finally?
And how much does he live while he lives?
We fret and ask so many questions –
then when it comes to us
the answer is so simple.

A man lives for as long as we carry him inside us,
for as long as we carry the harvest of his dreams,
for as long as we ourselves live,
holding memories in common, a man lives.

His lover will carry his man's scent, his touch;
his children will carry the weight of his love.
One friend will carry his arguments,
another will hum his favourite tunes,
another will still share his terrors.

And the days will pass with baffled faces,
then the weeks, then the months,
then there will be a day when no question is asked,
and the knots of grief will loosen in the stomach,
and the puffed faces will calm.
And on that day he will not have ceased,
but will have ceased to be separated by death.
How long does a man live, finally?

A man lives so many different lengths of time.

JOHN MILTON

'When I consider how my light is spent'

When I consider how my light is spent,
  Ere half my days, in this dark world and wide,
  And that one talent which is death to hide,
  Lodged with me useless, though my soul more bent
To serve therewith my Maker, and present
  My true account, lest he returning chide,
  Doth God exact day labour, light denied,
  I fondly ask; but patience to prevent
That murmur, soon replies, God doth not need
  Either man's work or his own gifts; who best
  Bear his mild yoke, they serve him best; his state
Is kingly. Thousands at his bidding speed
  And post o'er land and ocean without rest:
  They also serve who only stand and wait.

PERCY BYSSHE SHELLEY

Love's Philosophy

The fountains mingle with the river
And the rivers with the ocean,
The winds of heaven mix for ever
With a sweet emotion;
Nothing in the world is single,
All things by a law divine
In one another's being mingle –
Why not I with thine?

See the mountain's kiss high heaven
And the waves clasp one another;
No sister-flower would be forgiven
If it disdain'd its brother:

And the sunlight clasps the earth,
And the moonbeams kiss the sea –
What are all these kissings worth,
If thou kiss not me?

WALTER DE LA MARE

The Listeners

'Is there anybody there?' said the Traveller,
 Knocking on the moonlit door;
And his horse in the silence champed the grasses
 Of the forest's ferny floor:
And a bird flew up out of the turret,
 Above the Traveller's head:
And he smote upon the door again a second time;
 'Is there anybody there?' he said.
But no one descended to the Traveller;
 No head from the leaf-fringed sill
Leaned over and looked into his grey eyes,
 Where he stood perplexed and still.
But only a host of phantom listeners
 That dwelt in the lone house then
Stood listening in the quiet of the moonlight
 To that voice from the world of men:
Stood thronging the faint moonbeams on the dark stair,
 That goes down to the empty hall,
Hearkening in an air stirred and shaken
 By the lonely Traveller's call.
And he felt in his heart their strangeness,
 Their stillness answering his cry,
While his horse moved, cropping the dark turf,
 'Neath the starred and leafy sky;
For he suddenly smote on the door, even
 Louder, and lifted his head: –
'Tell them I came, and no one answered,
 That I kept my word,' he said.

Never the least stir made the listeners,
 Though every word he spake
Fell echoing through the shadowiness of the still
  house
 From the one man left awake:
Ay, they heard his foot upon the stirrup,
 And the sound of iron on stone,
And how the silence surged softly backward,
 When the plunging hoofs were gone.

RUDYARD KIPLING

The Way through the Woods

They shut the road through the woods
Seventy years ago.
Weather and rain have undone it again,
And now you would never know
There was once a road through the woods
Before they planted the trees.
It is underneath the coppice and heath
And the thin anemones.
Only the keeper sees
That, where the ring-dove broods,
And the badgers roll at ease,
There was once a road through the woods.

Yet, if you enter the woods
Of a summer evening late,
When the night-air cools on the trout-ringed pools
Where the otter whistles his mate,
(They fear not men in the woods,
Because they see so few.)
You will hear the beat of a horse's feet,
And the swish of a skirt in the dew,
Steadily cantering through
The misty solitudes,
As though they perfectly knew
The old lost road through the woods . . .
But there is no road through the woods.

WILLIAM SHAKESPEARE

from *King Lear* (Act V, Scene iii)

Enter Lear with Cordelia in his arms,
followed by Second Officer and others

LEAR:
Howl, howl, howl! O, you are men of stones!
Had I your tongues and eyes I'd use them so
That heaven's vault should crack. She's gone for ever.
I know when one is dead and when one lives;
She's dead as earth. Lend me a looking-glass;
If that her breath will mist or stain the stone,
Why then she lives.
KENT: Is this the promised end?
EDGAR:
Or image of that horror?

SAINT FRANCIS OF ASSISI

'Lord, make me an instrument of your peace.'

Lord, make me an instrument of your peace.
Where there is hatred, let me sow love;
where there is injury, pardon;
where there is doubt, faith;
where there is despair, hope;
where there is darkness, light;
and where there is sadness, joy.

O Divine Master, grant that I may not so much seek
to be consoled as to console;
to be understood as to understand;
to be loved as to love.
For it is in giving that we receive;
it is in pardoning that we are pardoned;
and it is in dying that we are born to eternal life.
    Amen

EMILY BRONTË

No coward soul is mine
No trembler in the world's storm-troubled sphere
I see Heaven's glories shine
And Faith shines equal arming me from Fear

O God within my breast
Almighty ever-present Deity
Life, that in me hast rest
As I Undying Life, have power in thee

Vain are the thousand creeds
That move men's hearts, unutterably vain,
Worthless as withered weeds
Or idlest froth amid the boundless main

To waken doubt in one
Holding so fast by thy infinity
So surely anchored on
The steadfast rock of Immortality

With wide-embracing love
Thy spirit animates eternal years
Pervades and broods above,
Changes, sustains, dissolves, creates and rears

Though Earth and moon were gone
And suns and universes ceased to be
And thou wert left alone
Every Existence would exist in thee

There is not room for Death
Nor atom that his might could render void
Since thou art Being and Breath
And what thou art may never be destroyed ·

PRIMO LEVI

(translated by Ruth Feldman)

To My Friends

Dear friends, and here I say friends
In the broad sense of the word:
Wife, sister, associates, relatives,
Schoolmates of both sexes,
People seen only once
Or frequented all my life;
Provided that between us, for at least a moment,
A line has been stretched,
A well-defined bond.

I speak for you, companions of a crowded
Road, not without its difficulties,
And for you too, who have lost
Soul, courage, the desire to live;
Or no one, or someone, or perhaps only one
    person, or you
Who are reading me: remember the time
Before the wax hardened,
When everyone was like a seal.
Each of us bears the imprint
Of a friend met along the way;
In each the trace of each.
For good or evil
In wisdom or in folly
Everyone stamped by everyone.

Now that the time crowds in
And the undertakings are finished,
To all of you the humble wish
That autumn will be long and mild.

Not Waving But Drowning

Nobody heard him, the dead man,
But still he lay moaning:
I was much further out than you thought
And not waving but drowning.

Poor chap, he always loved larking
And now he's dead
It must have been too cold for him his heart gave way,
They said.

Oh, no no no, it was too cold always
(Still the dead one lay moaning)
I was much too far out all my life
And not waving but drowning.

Pad, pad

I always remember your beautiful flowers
And the beautiful kimono you wore
When you sat on the couch
With that tigerish crouch
And told me you loved me no more.

What I cannot remember is how I felt when you were
    unkind
All I know is, if you were unkind now I should not mind.
Ah me, the power to feel exaggerated, angry and sad
The years have taken from me. Softly I go now, pad pad.

JOHN KEATS

To Autumn

Season of mists and mellow fruitfulness,
  Close bosom-friend of the maturing sun;
Conspiring with him how to load and bless
  With fruit the vines that round the thatch-eaves run;
To bend with apples the mossed cottage-trees,
  And fill all fruit with ripeness to the core;
    To swell the gourd, and plump the hazel shells
  With a sweet kernel; to set budding more,
And still more, later flowers for the bees,
Until they think warm days will never cease,
  For Summer has o'er-brimmed their clammy cells.

Who hath not seen thee oft amid thy store?
  Sometimes whoever seeks abroad may find
Thee sitting careless on a granary floor,
  Thy hair soft-lifted by the winnowing wind;
Or on a half-reaped furrow sound asleep,
  Drowsed with the fume of poppies, while thy hook
    Spares the next swath and all its twinèd flowers:
  And sometimes like a gleaner thou dost keep
Steady thy laden head across a brook;
Or by a cider-press, with patient look,
  Thou watchest the last oozings, hours by hours.

Where are the songs of Spring? Ay, where are they?
  Think not of them, thou hast thy music too –
While barrèd clouds bloom the soft-dying day,
  And touch the stubble-plains with rosy hue;
Then in a wailful choir the small gnats mourn
  Among the river shallows, borne aloft

Or sinking as the light wind lives or dies;
 And full-grown lambs loud bleat from hilly bourn;
Hedge-crickets sing; and now with treble soft
The red-breast whistles from a garden croft;
 And gathering swallows twitter in the skies.

CHRISTINA ROSSETTI

Remember

Remember me when I am gone away,
 Gone far away into the silent land;
 When you can no more hold me by the hand,
Nor I half turn to go yet turning stay.
Remember me when no more day by day
 You tell me of our future that you planned:
 Only remember me; you understand
It will be late to counsel then or pray.
Yet if you should forget me for a while
 And afterwards remember, do not grieve:
 For if the darkness and corruption leave
 A vestige of the thoughts that once I had,
Better by far you should forget and smile
 Than that you should remember and be sad.

Leisure

What is this life if, full of care,
We have no time to stand and stare.

No time to stand beneath the boughs
And stare as long as sheep or cows.

No time to see, when woods we pass,
Where squirrels hide their nuts in grass.

No time to see, in broad daylight,
Streams full of stars like skies at night.

No time to turn at Beauty's glance,
And watch her feet, how they can dance.

No time to wait till her mouth can
Enrich that smile her eyes began.

A poor life this if, full of care,
We have no time to stand and stare.

The Sick Rose

O Rose thou art sick
The invisible worm,
That flies in the night
In the howling storm:

Hath found out thy bed
Of crimson joy:
And his dark secret love
Does thy life destroy.

WILLIAM SHAKESPEARE

Sonnet 29

When, in disgrace with fortune and men's eyes,
I all alone beweep my outcast state,
And trouble deaf heaven with my bootless cries,
And look upon myself, and curse my fate,
Wishing me like to one more rich in hope,
Featured like him, like him with friends possessed,
Desiring this man's art and that man's scope,
With what I most enjoy contented least;
Yet in these thoughts myself almost despising,
Haply I think on thee – and then my state,
Like to the lark at break of day arising
From sullen earth, sings hymns at heaven's gate;
For thy sweet love rememb'red such wealth brings
That then I scorn to change my state with kings.

WILLIAM SHAKESPEARE

Sonnet 30

When to the sessions of sweet silent thought
I summon up remembrance of things past,
I sigh the lack of many a thing I sought,
And with old woes new wail my dear time's waste;
Then can I drown an eye, unused to flow,
For precious friends hid in death's dateless night,
And weep afresh love's long since cancelled woe,
And moan th'expense of many a vanished sight;
Then can I grieve at grievances foregone,
And heavily from woe to woe tell o'er
The sad account of fore-bemoanèd moan,
Which I new pay as if not paid before.
  But if the while I think on thee, dear friend,
  All losses are restored and sorrows end.

WILLIAM SHAKESPEARE

Sonnet 73

That time of year thou mayst in me behold
When yellow leaves, or none, or few, do hang
Upon those boughs which shake against the cold,
Bare ruined choirs where late the sweet birds sang.
In me thou seest the twilight of such day
As after sunset fadeth in the west,
Which by and by black night doth take away,
Death's second self, that seals up all in rest.
In me thou seest the glowing of such fire
That on the ashes of his youth doth lie,
As the deathbed whereon it must expire,
Consumed with that which it was nourished by.
   This thou perceiv'st, which makes thy love more
      strong,
   To love that well which thou must leave ere long.

WILLIAM HALL

from *Memories of a Decoy*

Where ducks by scores travers'd the fens,
coots, didappers, rails, waterhens;
combin'd with eggs, to change our pot,
two furlongs circle the spot;
fowl, fish all kinds, the table grac'd
all caught within the self same space;
as with revolved, in season fed,
the surplus found us salt and bread;
your humble servant, now your penman,
liv'd thus a simple, full-bred fenman.

EMILY DICKINSON

'I'm Nobody! Who are you?'

I'm Nobody! Who are you?
Are you – Nobody – Too?
Then there's a pair of us?
Don't tell! they'd advertise – you know!

How dreary – to be – Somebody!
How public – like a Frog –
To tell one's name – the livelong June –
To an admiring Bog!

EMILY DICKINSON

'After great pain, a formal feeling comes –'

After great pain, a formal feeling comes –
The Nerves sit ceremonious, like Tombs –
The stiff Heart questions was it He, that bore,
And Yesterday, or Centuries before?

The Feet, mechanical, go round –
Of Ground, or Air, or Ought –
A Wooden way
Regardless grown,
A Quartz contentment, like a stone –

This is the Hour of Lead –
Remembered, if outlived,
As Freezing persons, recollect the Snow –
First – Chill – then Stupor – then the letting go –

ALFRED, LORD TENNYSON

from *In Memoriam A. H. H.*

VII

Dark house, by which once more I stand
  Here in the long unlovely street,
  Doors, where my heart was used to beat
So quickly, waiting for a hand,

A hand that can be clasped no more –
  Behold me, for I cannot sleep,
  And like a guilty thing I creep
At earliest morning to the door.

He is not here; but far away
  The noise of life begins again,
  And ghastly through the drizzling rain
On the bald street breaks the blank day.

LOUIS MACNEICE

The Sunlight on the Garden

The sunlight on the garden
Hardens and grows cold,
We cannot cage the minute
Within its nets of gold,
When all is told
We cannot beg for pardon.

Our freedom as free lances
Advances towards its end;
The earth compels, upon it
Sonnets and birds descend;
And soon, my friend,
We shall have no time for dances.

The sky was good for flying
Defying the church bells
And every evil iron
Siren and what it tells:
The earth compels,
We are dying, Egypt, dying

And not expecting pardon,
Hardened in heart anew,
But glad to have sat under
Thunder and rain with you,
And grateful too
For sunlight on the garden.

HENRY VAUGHAN

Man

1

Weighing the steadfastness and state
Of some mean things which here below reside,
Where birds like watchful clocks the noiseless date
    And intercourse of times divide,
Where bees at night get home and hive, and flow'rs
      Early, as well as late,
Rise with the sun, and set in the same bow'rs;

2

'I would' (said I) 'my God would give
The staidness of these things to man!' For these
To his divine appointments ever cleave,
    And no new business breaks their peace;
The birds nor sow, nor reap, yet sup and dine;
      The flow'rs without clothes live,
Yet Solomon was never dressed so fine.

3

Man hath still either toys or care;
He hath no root, nor to one place is tied,
But ever restless and irregular
    About this earth doth run and ride;
He knows he hath a home, but scarce knows where,
      He says it is so far
That he hath quite forgot how to go there.

4

He knocks at all doors, strays and roams,
Nay, hath not so much wit as some stones have
Which in the darkest nights point to their homes,
    By some hid sense their maker gave;
Man is the shuttle, to whose winding quest
      And passage through these looms
God ordered motion, but ordained no rest.

WALT WHITMAN

from *The Wound Dresser*

I

An old man bending I come among new faces,
Years looking backward resuming in answer to children,
Come tell us old man, as from young men and maidens that
 love me,
(Arous'd and angry, I'd thought to beat the alarum, and
 urge relentless war,
But soon my fingers fail'd me, my face droop'd and I
 resign'd myself,
To sit by the wounded and soothe them, or silently watch
 the dead;)
Years hence of these scenes, of these furious passions, these
 chances,
Of unsurpass'd heroes (was one side so brave? the other was
 equally brave;)
Now be witness again, paint the mightiest armies of earth,
Of those armies so rapid so wondrous what saw you to tell
 us?
What stays with you latest and deepest? of curious panics,
Of hard-fought engagements or sieges tremendous what
 deepest remains?

WALT WHITMAN

I Saw in Louisiana a Live-Oak Growing

I saw in Louisiana a live-oak growing,
All alone stood it and the moss hung down from the
    branches,
Without any companion it grew there uttering joyous leaves
    of dark green,
And its look, rude, unbending, lusty, made me think of
    myself,
But I wonder'd how it could utter joyous leaves standing
    alone there without its friend near, for I knew I could not,
And I broke off a twig with a certain number of leaves upon
    it, and twined around it a little moss,
And brought it away, and I have placed it in sight in my
    room,
It is not needed to remind me as of my own dear friends,
(For I believe lately I think of little else than of them,)
Yet it remains to me a curious token, it makes me think of
    manly love;
For all that, and though the live-oak glistens there in
    Louisiana solitary in a wide flat space,
Uttering joyous leaves all its life without a friend a lover near,
I know very well I could not.

Acknowledgements

The publishers gratefully acknowledge permission to reprint copyright material in this book as follows:

'Still I Rise' and 'Impeccable Conception' from *The Complete Collected Poems of Maya Angelou* (Virago, 1994). Copyright © Maya Angelou, 1978, 1983. Reprinted by permission of Virago, an imprint of Little, Brown Book Group.

'The Wanderer', 'As I Walked Out One Evening', 'Their Lonely Betters', 'Night Mail', 'Lullaby' and 'Stop All the Clocks' from *W.H. Auden: Collected Shorter Poems* (Faber & Faber, 1966). Copyright © W. H. Auden, 1966. Reprinted by permission of Faber & Faber Ltd.

'In Our Year 1941 My Letter to You Mother Africa' and 'On an Afternoon Train from Purley to Victoria, 1955' from *Hot Earth Cold Earth* by James Berry (Bloodaxe, 1995). Copyright © James Berry, 1985, 1995. Reprinted by permission of Bloodaxe Books Ltd.

'Dream Song 14' and 'Dream Song 312' from *77 Dream Songs* by John Berryman (Faber & Faber, 1964). Copyright © 1959, 1962, 1963, 1964, 1965, 1966, 1967, 1968, 1969 the Estate of John Berryman. Reprinted by permission of Faber & Faber Ltd.

'Choosing a Mast' and 'The Sisters' from *Collected Poems of Roy Campbell*, published by Ad Donker Publishers (Pty) Ltd,

Index of Titles and First Lines

'96 65

' "A cold coming we had of it." ' 10
A Dream 30
A Drunk Man Looks at the Thistle 127
'A great bird landed here.' 132
A Man's a Man for A' That 122
A Poison Tree 139
A Red, Red Rose 121
'A tail behind, a trunk in front' 190
Ae Fond Kiss 124
'Ae fond kiss, and then we sever;' 124
'After great pain a formal feeling comes –' 247
'After hot loveless nights, when cold winds stream' 176
After the funeral 84
'After the funeral, mule praises, brays' 84
An Arundel Tomb 62
'An old man bending I come among new faces' 252
And death shall have no dominion 92
'And death shall have no dominion.' 92
'And did those feet in ancient time' 138
'And did you get what' 199
Ariel 74
Arthur 182
'As I listened from a beach-chair in the shade' 37
As I Walked Out One Evening 35
'As I walked out one evening' 35
'As to some lovely temple, tenantless' 219

Belfast Confetti 117
Break, Break, Break 226

'Break, break, break' 226
'Bringing their frozen swords, their salt-bleached eyes' 131

'Candy' 181
Casting and Gathering 68
Ceasefire 114
Chaplinesque 29
Choosing a Mast 177
Civil Lies 157
'come,gaze with me upon this dome' 26
Comfort 211

'Dark house, by which once more I Stand' 248
'Dear friends, and here I say friends' 327
'Dear Teacher' 157
Desideria 216
Dirge Without Music 221
Do not go gentle into that good night 91
'Do not go gentle into that good night' 91
'Doom is dark and deeper than any sea-dingle.' 34
'Douglass was someone who' 175
Dover Beach 21
Down by the Salley Gardens 94
'Down by the salley gardens my love and I did meet' 94
Dream Song 14 43
Dream Song 312 44
'Droning a drowsy syncopated tune' 167

Easter, 1916 98
Enosis 215

'Fair fa' your honest, sonsie face' 118
Fern Hill 89
Frederick Douglass: 1817–1895 175
Freedom 174
'Freedom will not come' 174
'From Cocoon forth a Butterfly' 144
From Number Nine, Penwiper Mews 189
'From Number Nine, Penwiper Mews' 189

'Good Morning – Midnight –' 146
'Grey over Riddrie the clouds piled up' 125

Grief 214
Growing Old 218

Hamlet 45
'Have you dug the spill' 170
'He ceased, and next him Moloch, sceptred king' 142
'He thought he saw an elephant' 185
'Hello, she said, and startled me.' 156
Heptonstall Old Church 132
Her 166
'her sleek' 65
'Here are two pictures from my father's head –' 115
' "Hope" is the thing with feathers –' 145
'How do I love thee? Let me count the ways' 213
'How long is a man's life, finally?' 227
Howl 49
'Howl, howl, howl! O, you are men of stones!' 234

'I always remember your beautiful flowers' 238
'I am not resigned to the shutting away of loving hearts in' 221
'I can feel the tug' 112
'i carry your heart with me(i carry it in' 23
'I classed, appraising once' 209
'I had been told about her.' 166
'I have been in the meadows all day' 212
'I have been so great a lover: filled my days' 51
'I have done it again.' 70
'I have met them at close of day' 98
'I have moved to Dublin to have it out with you' 44
'I idly cut a parsley stalk' 40
'I leave me people, me land, me home' 161
'I'm Nobody! Who are you?' 246
'I met a lady poet' 150
'I place my hope in the water' 116
I Saw in Louisiana a Live-Oak Growing 253
'I saw in Louisiana a live-oak growing' 253
'I saw the best minds of my generation destroyed by madness' 49
'I sit' 151
'I tell you, hopeless grief is passionless' 214
'I've Eaten Many Strange and Scrumptious Dishes . . .' 187
'I've eaten many strange and scrumptious dishes in my time' 187
'I've known rivers' 168
'I wake and feel the fell of dark, not day.' 32

'I wander thro' each charter'd street' 137
'I was angry with my friend' 139
'I went out to the hazel wood' 95
'I will arise and go now, and go to Innisfree' 107
Impeccable Conception 150
In a Dark Time 42
'In a dark time, the eye begins to see' 42
In Memoriam A. H. H. 248
In my country 165
In my craft or sullen art 88
'In my craft or sullen art' 88
In Our Year 1941 My Letter to You Mother Africa 151
'In the old days with married women's stockings' 41
Irreparableness 212
" 'Is there anybody there?' said the Traveller" 231
'Is there for honest poverty' 122
'It is the cause, it is the cause , my soul' 140
'it may not always be so;and i say' 24

Jabberwocky 183
'Jamie made his landing in the world' 66
Jerusalem 138
Journey of the Magi 10
'Just now the lilac is in bloom' 54

King Billy 125
King Lear 234

La Figlia Che Piange 15
Lady Lazarus 70
Late Fragment 199
'Lay your sleeping head, my love' 203
Leisure 241
'Let us go then, you and I' 3
'Life, friends, is boring. We must not say so.' 43
'Light flows our war of mocking words, and yet' 18
'Light spreads darkly downwards from the high' 64
London 137
'Lord, make me an instrument of your peace' 235
Love (III) 205
Love bade me welcome; yet my soul drew back 205
'Love set you going like a fat gold watch.' 69
Loved Once 209

Love's Philosophy 230
Lullaby 203

Man 250
Mary Morison 120
'Matilda told such Dreadful Lies' 195
Matilda (Who Told Lies and Was Burned to Death) 195
Memories of a Decoy 246
Morning Song 69
Mother, Summer, I 224
'My mother, who hates thunderstorms' 224
'"My name is Felix and I am a poet."' 28
'My own heart let me more have pity on; let' 33
My People 180
'My people' 180

'Nautilus Island's hermit' 47
Night Mail 38
'No coward soul is mine' 236
No Second Troy 108
'No worst, there is none. Pitched past pitch of grief' 31
'Nobody heard him, the dead man' 238
Not in Vain 207
Not Waving But Drowning 238
'Now as I was young and easy under the apple boughs' 89

'O Mary, at thy window be!' 120
'O my Luve is like a red, red rose' 121
'O Rose thou are sick' 242
'O, what will you give me?' 93
Ode to a Haggis 118
Of Course When They Ask for Poems About the 'Realities' of Black
    Women 162
'Of manly disposition was the youth' 79
'Of man's first disobedience, and the fruit' 141
On a Midsummer Eve 40
On an Afternoon Train from Purley to Victoria, 1955 156
On Raglan Road 110
'On Raglan Road on an autumn day I met her first and knew' 110
'Once a dream did weave a shade' 30
'one's not half two. It's two are halves of one:' 25
Othello 140

Pad, pad 238
Paradise Lost; Book I 141
Paradise Lost; Book II 142
Perfect Day 27
Poets Anonymous 28
Preludes 16
Punishment 112
Put Forth Thy Leaf 206
'Put forth thy leaf, thou lofty plane' 206
'Put in mind of his own father and moved to tears' 114

Reflections on Ice-breaking 181
Remember 240
'Remember me when I am gone away' 240
Requiem 182
Rhapsody on a Windy Night 12

'Say not the struggle nought availeth' 207
Scotland Small? 130
'Scotland small? Our multiform, our infinite Scotland *small*?' 130
'Seasons of mists and mellow fruitfulness' 239
'Side by side, their faces blurred' 62
Skunk Hour 47
Snow 111
So Many Different Lengths of Time 227
Song for a Dark Girl 169
Sonnet 29 243
Sonnet 30 244
Sonnet 73 245
Sonnets from the Portuguese 213
'Speak low to me, my saviour, low and sweet' 211
'Stand on the highest pavement of the stair –' 15
'Stasis in darkness.' 74
Stevie Scared 194
'Stevie Scared, scared of the dark' 194
Still I Rise 148
Stop All the Clocks 204
'Stop all the clocks, cut off the telephone' 204
'Suddenly as the riot squad moved in, it was raining exclamation
    marks' 117
'Surprised by joy—impatient as the wind' 216
'Swear by what the Sages spoke' 101

'Take some Picts, Celts and Silures' 159
'That day waz' 158
'That time of year thou mayst in me behold' 245
'That Whitsun, I was late getting away:' 59
The Bells of Rhymney 93
The British 159
The Buried Life 18
The Cow 181
'The Cow is of the bovine ilk' 181
The Crocodile or, Public Decency 191
The Elephant or, The Force of Habit 190
The force that through the green fuse 83
'The force that through the green fuse drives the flower' 83
'The fountains mingle with the river' 230
The Great Lover 51
The hunchback in the park 86
'The hunchback in the park' 86
'The instructor said' 172
The Ivy Crown 200
The Lake Isle of Innisfree 107
The Language Issue 116
'The language that but sparely floo'ers' 127
The Libertine 41
The Listeners 231
The Love Song of Alfred J. Prufrock 3
The Mad Gardener's Song 185
The Mower 225
'The mower stalled, twice; kneeling, I found' 225
The Negro Speaks of Rivers 168
The Old Vicarage, Granchester 54
The One Hope 208
The Oven Bird 223
The Owl and the Pussy-Cat 193
'The Owl and the Pussy-cat went to sea' 193
'The room was suddenly rich and the great bay-window was' 111
'The sea is calm to-night.' 21
The Second Coming 109
The Sick Rose 242
The Sisters 176
The Skunk 67
The Song of the Happy Shepherd 105
The Song of Wandering Aengus 95
The Sunlight on the Garden 249

'The sunlight on the garden' 249
The Thread 66
'The trees are in their autumn beauty' 96
The Turtle 182
'The turtle lives 'twixt plated decks' 182
The Wanderer 34
The Warriors of the North 131
The Way through the Woods 233
The Weary Blues 167
The Whitsun Weddings 59
'The whole process is a lie' 200
The Wild Swans at Coole 96
'The winter evening settles down' 16
'The woods of Arcady are dead' 105
The Wound Dresser 252
Their Lonely Betters 37
Theme for English B 172
'There is a singer everyone has heard' 223
'There was a young belle of old Natchez' 182
'There was an old man of Calcutta' 182
There's a Rather Odd Couple in Herts 189
'There's a rather odd couple in Herts' 189
'They fuck you up, your mum and dad.' 61
'They shut the road through the woods' 233
This Be the Verse 61
'This is the Night Mail crossing the Border' 38
'This mast, new-shaved, through whom I rive the ropes' 177
'Though some at my aversion smile' 191
'Thought is deeper than all speech' 215
'Time does not bring relief; you all have lied' 220
''Tis good – the looking back on Grief –' 147
To Autumn 239
'To be, or not to be – that is the question' 45
To My Friends 237
'Today was one of the best days of my life.' 27
Try to praise the mutilated world. 217
'Try to praise the mutilated world.' 217
'Turning and turning in the widening gyre' 109
''Twas brillig, and the slithy toves' 183
'Twelve o'clock.' 12

Under Ben Bulben 101
'Up, black, striped and demasked like the chasuble' 67

Walking Black Home 158
'walking by the waters' 165
'Way Down South in Dixie' 169
'We make our meek adjustments' 29
'Webster was much possessed by death' 8
'Weighing the Steadfastness and state' 250
'What is it to grow old?' 218
'What is this life if, full of care' 241
'What they really want' 162
'When I consider how my light is spent' 229
'When in disgrace with fortune and men's eyes' 243
'When to the sessions of sweet silent thought' 244
'When vain desire at last and vain regret' 208
When You Are Old 222
'When you are old and grey and full of sleep' 222
'Where ducks by scores travers'd the fens' 246
Wherever I Hang 161
Whispers of Immortality 8
'Why should I blame her that she filled my days' 108
Wounds 115

Y Gododdin 79
'Years and years ago, these sounds took sides:' 68
'You may write me down in history' 148
'You that love England, who have an ear for her music' 133